HEROES OF HISTORY

BENJAMIN FRANKLIN

Live Wire

HEROES OF HISTORY

BENJAMIN FRANKLIN

Live Wire

JANET & GEOFF BENGE

Emerald
Books

P.O. BOX 635, LYNNWOOD, WA 98046

Emerald Books are distributed through YWAM Publishing. For a full list of titles, including other great biographies, visit our website at www.ywampublishing.com or call 1-800-922-2143.

Benjamin Franklin: Live Wire
Copyright © 2005 by Janet and Geoff Benge

Published by Emerald Books
P.O. Box 635
Lynnwood, WA 98046

ISBN 978-1-932096-14-9 (paperback)
ISBN 978-1-932096-94-1 (e-book)

Library of Congress Cataloging-in-Publication Data
Benge, Janet, 1958–
    Benjamin Franklin : live wire / Janet and Geoff Benge.
      p. cm. — (Heroes of history)
    ISBN 1-932096-14-0
    1. Franklin, Benjamin, 1706–1790—Juvenile literature.
  2. Statesmen—United States—Biography—Juvenile literature.
  3. Inventors—United States—Biography—Juvenile literature.
  4. Scientists—United States—Biography—Juvenile literature.
  5. Printers—United States—Biography—Juvenile literature.
  I. Benge, Geoff, 1954– II. Title.
    E302.6.F8B4515 2005
    973.3'092—dc22   2004030213

Second printing 2013

Printed in the United States of America

HEROES OF HISTORY
Biographies

Abraham Lincoln
Alan Shepard
Benjamin Franklin
Christopher Columbus
Clara Barton
Davy Crockett
Daniel Boone
Douglas MacArthur
George Washington
George Washington Carver
Harriet Tubman
John Adams
John Smith
Laura Ingalls Wilder
Meriwether Lewis
Milton Hershey
Orville Wright
Ronald Reagan
Theodore Roosevelt
Thomas Edison
William Penn

All titles are available as e-books. Audiobooks and Unit Study Curriculum Guides are available for select biographies.

Visit www.ywampublishing.com or call 1-800-922-2143.

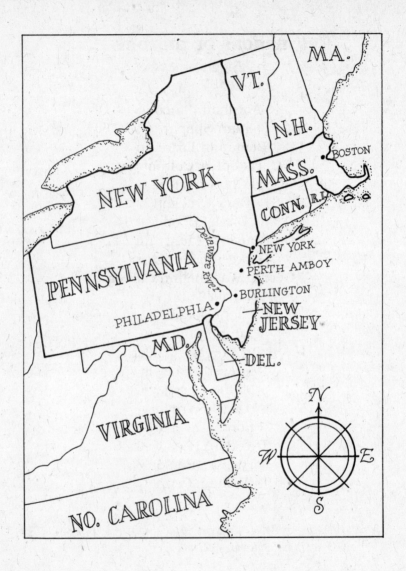

Contents

Chapter 1

Thunder and Lightning

W onderful," Ben Franklin mumbled to himself as he looked out his front window at the dark, bruised storm clouds rolling into Philadelphia. Then he grabbed the kite lying in the corner.

Just then Ben's twenty-two-year-old son William stepped into the room. "Looks like now is the time, don't you think so, Father?"

Ben nodded, and the two men headed for the door. Other people on Market Street were running for cover as the rain started to pelt them, but Ben and William made their way resolutely toward an open field on the outskirts of town. This was their kind of kite-flying weather.

Once they reached their destination, Ben took shelter in a small shepherd's hut while William launched the kite, running back and forth across the field until the kite took flight and climbed into the angry sky. Unlike a paper-covered kite, this kite was made from a large silk handkerchief stretched over a frame and would not disintegrate in the rain. A foot-long metal spike was lashed to the top of the kite, which was tethered to a long hemp cord. At the bottom of the hemp cord were a silk handkerchief for the kite flyer to hold and a brass key attached by a ribbon.

When all the cord was played out, William ran to his father, and as he handed him the cord, he yelled "good luck" over the deafening peals of thunder.

Ben stepped from the hut into the rain. He took the hemp cord from William and studied the sky. Finally he saw what he was looking for—a particularly low thundercloud rolling in toward them. He began guiding the kite toward the cloud, avoiding the forks of lightning that lit the sky. When the cloud had completely engulfed the kite in its grayness, Ben reached up and touched the brass key. He felt nothing. Disappointment swept over him. How could this be? This was not what he had expected. He was certain he was right about lightning being a form of electricity, and this experiment was supposed to prove it. But it hadn't. Could he be wrong? Or was there some flaw in the experiment?

Then Ben noticed that the loose threads on the now soaked hemp cord were standing on end. It could mean only one thing—they were electrically charged! As Ben carefully reached out to touch the key a second time, sparks arched between his knuckles and the brass key, and a jolt of electricity pulsed through him. It was an electric shock! Ben laughed with sheer delight. He had done it! He had proved that lightning and electricity were one and the same.

Ben touched the key a second time to double-check himself. Another jolt of electricity pulsed through his body. There could be no doubting the result of his experiment. Ben quickly began to reel in the kite. His experiment was over. He had discovered the answer to a question that had vexed humans for thousands of years: what was the true nature of lightning?

As he made his way home, Ben felt the full impact of what he had just done. Fifty years earlier Sir Isaac Newton had hypothesized that lightning was electrical in nature. Now Ben had confirmed that with a scientific experiment. It was an extraordinary accomplishment for any scientist, but Ben knew it was even more amazing for him, since he was not a trained scientist. He had come from a family of soap and candle makers in Boston. And although he had gone to school for only two years, he had continued educating himself through reading and experimenting and had now made an important discovery through one of those experiments.

As Ben walked home with William through the muddy streets of Philadelphia, his mind slipped back to his boyhood in Boston, where his love of science and learning had first surfaced.

Chapter 2

Soap and Candles

The coins in seven-year-old Ben Franklin's pocket jangled as Ben strode down the cobbled Boston street toward the toy shop. Ben's gray eyes sparkled as he thought how generous his father's friend had been to drop the coins into his pocket, and he could hardly wait to spend them. As Ben made his way along the narrow street, a pig careened past him, nearly knocking him into the open gutter that ran down the middle of the road. As he struggled to regain his balance, Ben heard a distinctive sound. It was the sweet, high-pitched sound of a tin whistle. Then he spotted a boy a few years older than he playing the whistle. Suddenly Ben knew he had to have that whistle. Without thinking, he reached into his pocket, pulled out all the coins, and offered them to the boy in exchange for the whistle. The boy snatched the coins from Ben, handed over the whistle, and ran off down the street.

Ben cradled the whistle in his hands as he ran home to show his family the amazing new toy. A minute later he rounded the corner of Union Street and sprinted down to Hanover Street, where his family's new house was located. He could hardly wait to make his grand entrance.

Ben marched from room to room, blowing what he thought was a wonderful tune. But he soon discovered that his playing was having the opposite effect from the one he had anticipated. His brother Thomas and his sisters Sarah and Lydia glared at him and plugged their ears. Even the family dog began to yelp and holler at the noise. Undeterred, Ben kept playing until he heard baby Jane wailing from her crib. His mother turned to him, her hands on her hips.

"Ben, you must stop that terrible noise at once," Abiah Franklin demanded.

"But it's my new whistle. Don't you like to hear it?" Ben asked.

"Maybe outside," his mother said in a softer voice. "It is an instrument for playing outdoors on the Commons, not here in the house."

"Let me see this new whistle," Ben's father, Josiah, said as he sat by the fire, reading a newspaper.

Ben proudly passed the instrument to his father.

"And how much did you pay for it?" Josiah Franklin asked.

"I saw a boy playing it on the street, and I gave him all the coins I had in my pocket."

"You what?" his father said incredulously. "But you could have bought a brand-new one for a quarter of that price! What were you thinking?"

Ben heard someone chuckling. He turned around just as his mother and siblings burst out laughing. He felt his face turning red and his stomach heaving. Tears rolled down his cheeks as he thought about all the other things he could have bought with the money he overpaid for the whistle. He ran to his bedroom and threw the tin whistle under his bed, promising himself that he would never again "give too much for a whistle."

Ben did take his whistle to the Commons sometimes, but he could never play it without thinking about how he had made a fool of himself and wasted his money as well.

In the Franklins' Puritan New England home, wasting money was a grave sin. And as Ben had learned, it was assumed that he would become the family expert on sin and other religious matters. Ben's father had told him that this was because of his birth. Ben was fourteenth of seventeen children born to Josiah Franklin and his first wife, Anne, and second wife, Abiah. And since Ben was the tenth of ten sons, his father had informed him that he had decided that as a tithe Ben should become a clergyman. Ben was not excited about this, since church seemed very boring to him, but he was excited about attending Boston Grammar (Latin) School as the first part of his clergyman training. Ben's father had told Ben that he would have to attend grammar school and then attend Harvard University for four years before he could be ordained a minister. So in 1714, at age eight, Ben Franklin found himself starting school.

At Boston Grammar, Ben was soon learning to read and write in Latin and to read the Greek classics in their original language, subjects on which he would have to pass an examination to get into Harvard. Ben proved to be a good student with a quick mind. He had been reading since he was three years old, and he was soon top of his class.

Josiah Franklin was pleased with Ben's grades, as was Ben's Uncle Benjamin, who had just arrived from England. Uncle Benjamin was Ben's father's older brother. His wife and nine of his ten children had died, and he had decided to sail to Boston in the hopes that his last surviving son, Samuel, would follow. Ben's cousin Samuel was a cutler, and Uncle Benjamin thought that he could make a good living making scissors and knives in the colony.

Uncle Benjamin fascinated Ben. He brought many books with him from England and had created his own version of shorthand so that he could write down sermons as he heard them. This impressed Ben, who begged his uncle to teach him how to read and write the shorthand. Uncle Benjamin was happy to do so, and he even promised Ben that he would one day inherit his entire collection of leather-bound sermons written in the special shorthand.

Uncle Benjamin was also a great storyteller, and Ben spent many snowy nights listening to tales about his Franklin ancestors back in England. Ben particularly liked to hear about how his great-great-grandfather had secretly fastened a Protestant

English Bible under a stool during the cruel reign of Queen Mary I from 1553 to 1558. Bloody Mary, as the queen was soon nicknamed, took delight in having religious leaders who did not follow her Catholic beliefs burned at the stake. The only Bible she allowed in England was the official Catholic edition in Latin. Since the queen did not allow people to have copies of the Bible in English, Ben's great-great-grandfather had hidden his Bible under the stool, and when he wanted to read it, he had one of his children stand guard at the door while he flipped over the stool and read it aloud to the family.

Not only did Ben like to be told stories, but he liked to read them for himself. His favorite was *Pilgrim's Progress* by John Bunyan. What particularly caught his interest was the way Bunyan used dialogue, or conversation between his characters, to help tell the story. Something about this approach seemed to make the story come alive for Ben as had no other story he had ever read. Ben's English teacher told him that John Bunyan was the first English writer to use dialogue in his storytelling.

A love of reading was a good attribute for a clergyman, but other aspects of Ben's personality were not quite so suited to the profession Ben's father had chosen for him. Ben found this out one day when he overheard his father talking to Uncle Benjamin.

"The boy has a quick mind," Ben heard his father say, "but I doubt the depth of his piety to be a clergyman. He seems to have no patience for prayer. Why, he even suggested to me a way to speed up grace before each meal."

"Really?" his uncle replied.

"Yes," he heard his father go on. "I was nailing shut a barrel of salted meat for the winter, when the boy suggested I say grace over the whole barrel right then and there so that we would not have to waste time before each meal giving thanks! Do you see a boy with that sort of attitude becoming a minister?"

"I must say Ben loves to read the sermons I write down, but I think that has more to do with deciphering the shorthand than it does any desire to be pious. Maybe you are steering him into the wrong course, brother," Uncle Benjamin said.

On hearing this conversation, Ben was not surprised when soon afterward his father withdrew him from Boston Grammar and enrolled him in George Brownwell's School for Writing and Arithmetic. The goal of this school, which girls could also attend, was to train the students to read, write, and do arithmetic, skills they would need to become apprentices and tradesmen.

After Ben had attended George Brownwell's School for Writing and Arithmetic for one year, his father withdrew him from the school. Ben was now ten years old, and it was time for him to start working in the family soap- and candle-making business.

Josiah Franklin had already set two of Ben's older brothers up in their own soap- and candle-making businesses. And now that Ben was not going to be a clergyman, it seemed the obvious choice of profession for him as well. When Ben's father had come to Massachusetts from England in 1682, he had been a fabric dyer. But since the Puritans of

New England tended to wear dull-colored clothes, there was little need for dyers to produce brightly colored fabrics. So Josiah Franklin had taken up candle and soap making. And he had done well at this craft. He now had a contract to supply the night watchmen of Boston with candles, which were made in the workshop and sold from the small store that sat adjacent to the Franklin house on the corner of Union and Hanover Streets. Ben soon found himself spending twelve hours a day, six days a week, working alongside his father as he cut wicks, set up the molds for cast candles, sold soap, and ran errands.

After Ben had mastered the craft of making soap and candles, he found the work tedious. There was one job that Ben grew to loathe above all others. Once a week he took a wheelbarrow and made his way through the streets of Boston, collecting beef and sheep fat from the various butchers in town. In the summer, when the weather was hot, the putrefying smell of the rancid fat made Ben want to throw up. Once he managed to get the fat home, Ben would load it into large kettles and light fires under them. The heat would purify the fat into tallow, a process called rendering. Then the tallow was used to make the candles or was combined with lye to make soap. Regrettably for Ben, he soon discovered that no matter how hard he tried, he could not get rid of the smell of rendering fat from his clothes or off his skin.

As he labored away making soap and candles, Ben often thought about his brother Josiah, who as a boy had run away to sea. Ben's brother was twenty-one years older than he was and had recently returned home for a visit. Josiah told Ben exotic stories of his experiences among the islands of the Caribbean and in India and other far-off places. How Ben longed to visit such places far away from the drudgery of making candles and soap. But when he suggested to his father that he was considering going off to sea like his brother, his father's eyes narrowed. His father explained to Ben what a bad idea this would be, and how his future lay in making soap and candles or in some other trade that would provided a good living free from the perils of ocean voyages. And as if to underline his father's words, a letter arrived soon after informing the Franklin family that Josiah's ship had sunk in a howling storm and Josiah had been drowned. The news of Josiah's death seemed to make Ben's father more determined than ever to talk Ben out of going to sea. Despite his father's best efforts, Ben continued to feel the lure of a life at sea.

In the long summer evenings, to relieve his boredom, Ben would go fishing or swimming with his friends. On one particular night, as he and his friends stood ankle deep in mud among the mangroves along the shore of Boston Harbor, fishing for minnows, Ben spotted a pile of stones waiting to be used in the construction of a new home.

"Wouldn't it be great to have a jetty to stand on and fish from without all this mud?" Ben asked, pointing to the pile of rocks.

Within minutes the boys were busy moving the stones from the pile into the water to form a jetty.

In the moonlight Ben and the other boys admired their handiwork before heading home for bed.

The following day a mason came to talk to Ben's father. Ben watched the grim look that settled across his father's face, and he began to think fast. When the man left, Ben's father called him over.

"It seems that last night some boys removed a pile of rocks that were not theirs to build a jetty. And I am told that you were one of those boys. Is that true?"

A long silence followed.

"Well, what do you have to say for yourself, boy?" Ben's father said sternly.

Ben knew that there was no use denying it, so he used a different approach. He tried to convince his father that the jetty was good for the entire community, since anyone could now fish for minnows without getting his feet muddy.

"That may well be so," his father replied calmly, "but the stones were not yours to use. Nothing is useful that is not honest. Tonight after work, you and your friends must return all of the stones."

Besides liking to fish, Ben liked swimming. In fact, he was one of only a few boys who could both float and swim. Even most sailors did not know how to swim. One day while Ben was floating on his back in a nearby millpond, watching his tethered kite flying, he came up with an idea. He climbed out of the pond, untied the kite tether, and tugged the cord as he climbed back into the water. Then, still holding onto the kite, he floated on his back. Much to his delight, the wind pulled the kite and him with it across the pond. Ben was amazed at how fast his body skimmed along, and he soon attracted a crowd of young admirers. He became fascinated with finding other ways to move through the water faster. He experimented with a pair of wooden hand paddles that pushed more water out behind him as he swam, propelling him forward with greater speed. Ben carefully wrote down the various experiments he conducted and drew diagrams of them.

Still, Ben could pursue these interests only after work or on Sunday afternoons. The rest of the time he was stuck in the smelly soap- and candle-making shop. Much to Ben's relief, his father finally noticed how unhappy he was and offered to help Ben look for a trade that would better suit his inquiring mind.

Over the next several weeks, Ben and his father visited all of the tradesmen in Boston, looking for a more suitable job. As they made their way through the narrow, cobbled streets, Ben observed brick- layers, blacksmiths, cabinetmakers, roofers, brass workers, coopers, cobblers, millers, and leather work- ers at their trades. Although Ben was fascinated by what these men did, he could not see himself doing any of those things for the next five years, much less for the rest of his life.

By now Ben's cousin Samuel had established himself as a cutler in Boston, and for want of a bet- ter choice for his son, Josiah Franklin decided to apprentice Ben to him. Ben moved in with Samuel and began to learn the art of making knives and scissors. But after only a few days at this, Ben's father ordered Ben to pack up his things and move back home. Ben learned that Samuel had demanded he be paid a fee for taking Ben on as his apprentice, a practice that was normal back in England, where apprenticeships were controlled by powerful guilds, but was not done in the American colonies. This made Josiah furious, especially since Samuel's father, Uncle Benjamin, had been staying with the Franklins free of charge for four years.

Ben was rather relieved to be out from under his cousin's thumb, and the search for a new profession continued. A new option for Ben soon presented itself.

Years before, Ben's brother James, who was ten years older than Ben, had gone to England and learned the printing trade. Now he had returned to establish himself as a printer in Boston and was in need of someone to help him run the press. It was arranged that James would take on Ben as his apprentice. James agreed to teach Ben the craft of printing and to provide him with meals, clothes, and a place to live, which would serve as his pay. In return, Ben signed apprenticeship papers stating that he would work loyally for James, do whatever he was asked to do cheerfully and without complaint, and remain working for his brother for the next nine years. Ben calculated that he would be twenty-one before he was free to take on another job or move away. If he ran away to sea now, he would be violating the law and could be thrown in jail. It was a sobering thought for a twelve-year-old boy. Ben just hoped that he would like printing better than the other jobs he had tried his hand at.

Chapter 3

The Apprentice

James Franklin's print shop was located on Queen's Street, three blocks from the Franklin home and next door to the town jail. James was working hard to establish his new business and eke out a niche for himself among the four other printers in Boston, and he soon had Ben hard at work too. Ben did not mind this because printing newspapers and pamphlets involved a lot more interesting steps than making soap and candles.

Ben soon learned the basics. When a customer came to the print shop, the words he wanted printed were most often handwritten on paper. Sometimes they were just an idea in his head, and the printer had to write them down and edit them for him. Once the words were finalized, James set them in cast-metal type, letter by letter, row upon row, in a large, flat frame, or plate, as it was called in the trade. Often four pages of type were laid out per plate. Then the type had to be proofread and the plates placed on the press, where ink was rolled over the cast-metal type. A sheet of paper was then laid over the type, and pressure was applied to transfer the image from the inked plate onto the paper. Each printed sheet was then taken from the press and laid aside to dry before it was cut or trimmed by a guillotine and the pages were bound together to form the final document.

It was often hard, backbreaking work, but as a result of his swimming and other physical activity, Ben had developed strong arms and shoulders and was soon lugging the heavy printing plates around two at a time. But the part of the job that Ben enjoyed most was helping customers write down exactly what they wanted to say and editing it for them. Sometimes a busy customer would actually let Ben do the writing.

Best of all, working for a printer gave Ben access to a lot of books to read. Often the apprentices to Boston booksellers would come to the print shop to collect books and other printed material. One of these apprentices was John Collins, and he and Ben soon struck up a friendship. John was several years older, and when Ben explained how much he loved to read, John offered to bring books for Ben to read in the evenings after the bookshop had closed. Ben would read the volume John brought overnight and return it early in the morning before the bookshop opened. It wasn't long before Ben was learning to get by on less and less sleep so that he could read these new books.

One of the books John loaned Ben was titled *The Way to Wealth*. Among other things, this book extolled the virtues of being a vegetarian, and as Ben thought about it, he realized that by becoming a vegetarian he could save a lot of money. He came up with a plan. Ben and James boarded with a family who lived nearby, and James paid the family extra to supply him and Ben with three meals a day. Ben asked James whether, if he gave up eating meat, James would be prepared to give him the money he spent on Ben's meals so that Ben could buy his own food? Much to Ben's delight, James said he would.

Now Ben had money of his own. He soon got into a routine of eating only bread and raisins and drinking water. This cost only a quarter of the food money, and Ben was able to spend the other three-quarters on books.

The new arrangement also gave Ben more time to read. Instead of walking from the print shop to the boardinghouse to eat his meals with James, Ben stayed behind and read while he ate his bread and raisins.

One day as Ben was busy working the press, Matthew Adams, a regular customer at the print shop, walked in. After talking to James for several minutes, Matthew beckoned to Ben.

"Every time I talk with you, I am greatly impressed by your inquisitiveness, lad," Matthew said.

"Thank you, sir," Ben replied politely.

"Since you are so inquisitive and such a voracious reader, I have decided to grant you access to the Adams family library. It's not the biggest private library in Boston, but I think you will find many books of interest to you there. You may take two at a time and exchange them on Sunday afternoons. How would that suit you?"

Ben hardly knew how to respond. He now had hundreds of new books to read at no cost to him! "Thank you, sir, ah...Mr. Adams," he finally stammered. "It is a great honor. I will take good care of the books."

Soon Ben was devouring books from the Adams family library, again sitting up through the night reading. The more Ben read, the more he began to think about writing his own stories and articles. So many ideas swirled around inside his head, and one lunchtime he decided to give writing a try. He took some scraps of paper from the waste pile and a quill pen, and before long he had composed a poem titled "The Lighthouse Tragedy," about the recent drowning of a local lighthouse keeper and his wife and small child. Ben was surprised at how easily the poem flowed, and so he tried again. This time his subject was Edward Teach, more commonly known as the pirate Blackbeard, who had been killed about a year before. Ben made the poem as dramatic as he could.

Will you hear of a bloody battle,
Lately fought upon the seas,
It will make your ears to rattle,

And your admiration cease.
Have you heard of Teach the Rover
And his knavery on the main,
How of gold he was a lover,
How he loved all ill-got gain.

Ben ended his poem describing the brutal death of Blackbeard.

Teach and Maynard on the quarter,
Fought it out most manfully;
Maynard's sword did cut him shorter,
Losing his head he there did die.

After he had spent some time polishing his poems, Ben nervously showed them to James. Much to his relief, James liked them and suggested that they print up the poems and sell them. Much to Ben's surprise, the poems sold well, especially "The Lighthouse Tragedy."

Given the success of the poems, it came as a shock to Ben when his father declared them awful. "They are like something the writers on Grub Street turn out," he said, referring to the street in London that was inhabited by impoverished writers and literary hacks. He also pointed out that there was no money to be made in writing ballads, and he suggested that Ben instead try his hand at a more respectable literary category. Although Ben was stung by his father's criticism, he wondered whether he had a point, and he turned his attention to a different form of writing—letters.

To sharpen his writing skills, Ben convinced John Collins that they should write letters to each other debating certain topics. Their first topic was the education of women. Ben took the side that women should be educated beyond basic reading and writing, while John argued that if a woman could read and write, that was enough. Back and forth the letters went, and as they did so, Ben could see that his points were logical but that John had a knack for writing in a more fluid style. It was an observation soon confirmed by Ben's father after reading a pile of letters Ben had left lying around the family home.

"I read several of these letters," he told Ben. "You have a good mind and argue well, but John has a much better writing style than you do. Look..." With that Josiah Franklin unfolded several of Ben's and John's letters and began comparing them.

Ben could have been insulted by his father's actions, but he was not. He knew that his father's critique was right; he did need to improve his writing style. But how?

As Ben pondered this question, he was given an issue of the *Spectator* to read. The *Spectator* was a journal published in London that was packed full of essays and other forms of lively writing. Ben read the whole issue from cover to cover. This was the kind of writing he wanted to produce. So he made a plan.

Each day Ben decided that he would reread one of the essays from the *Spectator* and think about how it was written. He would then recompose the main point of the essay in poem form. Then, several weeks later, when he had forgotten the exact wording of the essay, he would use the poem to construct his own essay, which he would then compare with the original essay in the *Spectator.*

This plan worked well, and soon Ben was giving himself new challenges. He would make notes on small slips of paper about the essay that he was reading. He would then put the notes away in a drawer. After a week or two had gone by, he would take out the notes, shuffle them so that they were no longer in order, and try to logically reconstruct the argument the writer of the essay was trying to make. Then once again he would rewrite the essay, trying to make it as good as or better than the original.

Within three months Ben could see that he had made a lot of progress. He had also made an interesting discovery along the way: sometimes using fewer words was more powerful than using a lot of them. This applied to speaking as well as writing. Being a young man with an opinion on just about everything, Ben was often accused of arguing too much. Now that he was more aware of how to use words, he decided to try talking less and listening more. As he debated with his family and friends, he made a point of asking them a few strategic questions rather than lecturing them about his own view on a matter. The result was startling. The people Ben debated often tied themselves in knots trying to answer his simple questions, saving Ben the effort of trying to convince them that their arguments were faulty. Ben decided he would always be a listener and a questioner rather than a debater who contradicted others.

In 1721, after Ben had been an apprentice printer for three years, James decided to start his own newspaper, which he named the *New England Courant*. Boston already had two other newspapers, both of which relied on the support of the postmaster for the various news stories they printed. Since being postmaster was a government position, these newspapers were careful not to criticize the colony's government, and especially not Governor Shute. Nor did these two newspapers attack Cotton Mather, Boston's leading Puritan, and his family. However, James was hotheaded enough not to care about challenging these leaders and government officials, and Ben sensed that the *New England Courant* would soon be in trouble.

Ben was right. After two editions the postmaster refused to supply the paper with any of the news that arrived in his office from England or the other colonies. Ben watched as James and some of his friends pondered what could be published in the paper. Finally they came up with a plan. The *New England Courant* would concentrate on satire, the art of trying to bring change through poking fun at public figures and government policies. It was a risky plan, but James was delighted to be able to write articles that would make the people of Boston take a long look at their community and its leaders.

The idea caught on, and soon Ben was occupied setting the type for the newspaper and printing it each week. When the copies of the paper were all printed, he sold them on street corners.

The *New England Courant* soon found a ready audience, and Ben noticed that this emboldened his brother. James began to write more scathing articles about the colonial government and Cotton Mather. Ben was not altogether surprised when, in 1722, James was arrested and thrown into jail for his writing. Before the governor let James go, James had to apologize for the offending remarks and produce a doctor's certificate stating that his imprisonment was damaging his health.

Just as Ben expected, however, James continued writing the same things he had before, except this time he attacked the establishment through letters to the editor. He wrote the letters himself, using fake names such as "Abigail Afterwit," "Timothy Turnstone," "Harry Meanwell," and "Fanny Mournful" to get his point across. The letters were a great hit, and James encouraged his readers to write letters to the editor as well.

In April 1722 Ben had an idea. If readers could write letters to the editor, then so could he! He set to work one evening, writing under the name of "Mrs. Silence Dogood," the prim and proper widow of a New England vicar who had opinions on almost everything going on in the community. When he had finished the letter, Ben pushed it under the print shop door, where James would be sure to see it when he opened up in the morning.

When Ben arrived at the print shop, he was amazed to see how excited James was about the

Silence Dogood letter. And when James showed the letter to his friends, they all loved it too. Ben wished he could tell them that he had written it, but he knew that James would not publish it if he knew the truth. Ben had noticed over his five years as his brother's apprentice that James got jealous when Ben outshined him or proved him wrong on a point.

When James published Silence Dogood's letter in the next issue of the newspaper, many readers came into the print shop to ask James if they would be hearing from Silence again. Ben decided to seize the opportunity. From April to October he was kept busy secretly penning long letters from Silence Dogood as she criticized many of the goings-on in the community.

Finally, in October, Ben decided to tell James the truth. The letters had been so successful that Ben was sure that James would let him keep writing them. But he was wrong. Silence Dogood mysteriously left the area and was never heard from again in the *New England Courant*.

Ben was disappointed, but other, more important matters soon claimed his attention. James had again infuriated the colonial government. When someone close to the governor warned James that a warrant was out for his arrest, James fled into hiding. When the governor's men could not find him, they issued an order forbidding him to print another issue of the newspaper.

Since the newspaper provided most of the income for the print shop, this presented quite a problem, but James finally came up with a solution. When

Ben went to visit his brother, who was holed up in a friend's coal cellar, James explained that the order forbade *him* from publishing the *New England Courant*. It did not mean that the newspaper couldn't be published under someone else's name. Ben felt his pulse quicken as he realized that James meant for him to publish the *New England Courant* under his own name.

The scheme had just one problem. Ben was still James's apprentice, bound to work for him by contract until he was twenty-one years old. In the eyes of the law, as long as Ben was an apprentice to James, he, too, was barred from being the publisher of the newspaper. James, who'd had nothing else to think about while in hiding, had already come up with a solution to this dilemma. He offered to release Ben from the apprenticeship contract and sign a statement saying that Ben had completed the terms of his apprenticeship and was now a duly qualified printer.

Ben did not know what to think. One minute he was an apprentice with four years to go on his contract, and the next minute his brother was offering to free him from that contract and make him the publisher of a newspaper. But as Ben soon found out, the offer had a catch. James insisted that Ben secretly sign another contract that stated he was still James's apprentice. Ben reluctantly agreed to this condition.

The February 11, 1723, issue of the newspaper announced that James Franklin was no longer associated with producing the *New England Courant* and that his brother, Benjamin Franklin, was now the paper's publisher. At seventeen Ben found this to be quite an accomplishment, though he doubted that things would run smoothly. Despite having his own name on the newspaper's masthead, Ben was sure that his brother would have plenty to say about how the newspaper was run.

Once again Ben was right. Within days the two brothers were arguing about every aspect of how and what to print. Ben felt that he knew better, faster ways to do things, but even though he was not there to supervise things, James insisted that everything stay the same.

Finally, in September 1723, after a particularly bitter argument with James, Ben decided he'd had enough. He was tired of working for his brother for no pay and more abuse than he thought he should have to bear. He decided it was time for him to find work with another printer. There was just one catch: the secret contract Ben had signed meant that he was still legally James's apprentice. But as Ben thought about it, he realized that James could never produce the contract in court. If he did so, he would be admitting that he was still the real publisher of the newspaper and that Ben had just been a cover for him. That would put James in contempt of the court order not to publish the newspaper and would land him in even more serious trouble. James might have the contract, but what use was it if he could not show it to anyone?

Ben soon discovered that James had anticipated such a move and had convinced the other printers

in Boston not to hire him if he came seeking work.
This turn of events left Ben with few options. All the
printers in Massachusetts were located in Boston;
the only other printers Ben knew of were located in
far-off New York. So that is where Ben decided to
go. He never told his family what he was planning
as he sold some of his books to pay for passage to
New York.

Ben soon discovered another fact he had not
accounted for: no one under the age of twenty-one
could leave Massachusetts without his or her
father's permission. Ben, though, had come too far
to turn back now, and he looked for a way to get
around this latest problem. His friend John Collins
came to his rescue. John knew a ship's captain,
and he told the captain that Ben was in serious
trouble and needed to secretly leave Boston as soon
as possible. The captain agreed to let John smuggle
Ben aboard his ship, and within days of the argument with James, Ben watched as the coast of
Massachusetts disappeared from view. He felt a few
pangs of doubt as the ship sailed away. He had little money, no friends or family awaiting him at the
other end, and no idea whether he could actually
get a job in New York. But it was too late to turn
back. Massachusetts had already faded from view.
At seventeen years of age, Ben Franklin felt that he
was in charge of his own destiny.

Chapter 4

Philadelphia

A s he looked up at the billowing sails, Ben took stock of his assets: three dollars in coins, two sets of clothing—the clothes he was wearing and a Sunday set in his trunk—two books, his apprenticeship completion and discharge papers signed by his brother James, and his wits. His doubts had subsided now, and Ben smiled as he thought about what the future held for him. He planned to take a job in New York as a printer and buy as many books as he wanted with the money he earned. He had no plans to return home to Boston until he was well past his twenty-first birthday and had a silver watch and chain and money in his pocket with which to impress his family.

Two days after setting out from Boston, the sails of the ship hung listlessly against the mast. They

were becalmed near Block Island off the mouth
of Narragansett Bay. However, while they were
becalmed, the sailors were not idle. Ben watched as
they unrolled huge nets and slung them over the
side of the ship. Soon the nets were teeming with
cod and were pulled aboard. It wasn't long before
the tantalizing smell of frying fish reached Ben's
nose. The scent left him feeling conflicted. On the
one hand he loved fish as much as any other New
Englander, but on the other hand he was a vegetarian. He had stopped eating meat to save money,
but over the years he had grown proud that he did
not eat innocent animals who had never harmed
him in any way.

As Ben watched the cook gutting the fish in
preparation for cooking them, he noticed that some
of the bigger cod had smaller fish in their bellies.
Suddenly a light went on in Ben's mind. If fish
could eat each other, why couldn't he eat them as
well? The thought cheered Ben considerably, and
he picked up a plate and joined his fellow passengers for a delicious meal of the best Atlantic cod he
had ever eaten.

No sooner was the meal over than the wind began
to pick up again. The nets were soon rolled up and
stowed, and then the sailors trimmed the sails. Soon
they were again moving in a southwesterly direction.

A day later the ship dropped anchor in New York
harbor. Ben had never seen any other town but
Boston, and New York, nestled on the southern end
of Manhattan Island, was quite a sight. Ben did not
know a single person in the city, but that did not

worry him. He expected to find four or five print shops in town, and he was confident that at least one of them would hire him.

By the end of his first day in New York, Ben was stunned. He could scarcely believe it. Most of the people in town spoke Dutch, and there was not a single newspaper in the place—in any language. Ben did manage to locate one printer, a man named William Bradford, who explained to Ben that he did not have enough work to hire another man in his print shop. When Ben questioned him as to why he had not started a newspaper, William told Ben that New Yorkers were mainly merchants who did not have the time or interest to read about the outside world. Nor did they want to read printed sermons such as those the Puritans in New England liked to read in their papers.

Ben realized that he must have looked desperate, because William told him that his son Andrew was also a printer and was looking to hire a new employee to replace an assistant who had recently died. There was just one catch—Andrew Bradford lived one hundred miles away in Philadelphia.

That night, as Ben lay on a lumpy bed in a cheap hotel, he weighed his options. He had no skills other than printing, except perhaps basic candle making, but he hated the thought of trying to make a living at that again. And since there were no print jobs in New York, the best he could hope for was to find work on the docks loading and unloading ships. But that option had even less appeal than going back to candle making. In the end Ben had to admit to himself that the idea of moving on to Philadelphia did have its good points. For one thing, it was another hundred miles farther away from his family, lessening the possibility that he would be tracked down and forced to return to work for James in Boston. And for another thing, it would give him a chance to see another of the American colonies. As he finally drifted off to sleep, Ben promised himself that he would set out for Pennsylvania first thing in the morning.

Ben slept fitfully. The man in the next bed coughed and spluttered all night. At first light, Ben got up and headed off to find a boat to take him across the Hudson River. He soon came to regret boarding the cheapest boat he could find. The ferryman had little experience, and when a storm blew up, the rotten sail ripped to shreds. The waves drove the boat completely off course. To make matters worse, one of the passengers, a drunken Dutchman, was pitched overboard by a large wave. Ben was the only person looking in his direction at the time, and he reached his powerful arms over the side of the boat and grabbed the man by his hair. He pulled the man back aboard and laid him in the scuttle, where he fell sound asleep, leaving Ben and the other passengers to frantically bail water out of the boat.

Eventually the boat drifted near the shore of Long Island near the mouth of New York harbor, but the surf was too high and the coast too rocky to land safely. People on shore waved and signaled to the craft, but no one seemed willing to risk his life to help transfer the passengers to land. Instead the ferryman dropped anchor and waited out the storm.

Night fell, and a bottle of rum, which proved to be the only drink aboard, was passed from passenger to passenger. Soon everyone found somewhere to lie as they all spent a long, wet night bobbing about in the boat. As dawn lit the morning sky, the wind shifted to the east. One of the passengers had a linen sheet with him, and the ferryman was able to rig it up as a makeshift sail. Then, slowly, the ferry began to head toward its original destination—Perth Amboy in New Jersey.

That night, Ben finally set foot again on dry land, thirty-six hours after setting out on the two-hour ferry ride. Once ashore he followed some of the other passengers to the nearest inn and collapsed into bed. His stomach ached with hunger, and he was wet to the bone but grateful to be alive.

The next morning Ben ate a hearty breakfast and then set out on foot for Burlington, located on the Delaware River on the other side of New Jersey. He arrived there the following day, Saturday, only to learn that he had just missed the boat that he had planned to catch downriver to Philadelphia. The next boat was not due until Tuesday. Discouraged, Ben flopped down beside the river to think about what he should do. He had been sitting beside the Delaware River for about an hour when he spotted a boat making its way downstream. He called out to the vessel and soon learned that it was headed for Philadelphia and that there was room aboard for one more person. Ben could scarcely believe his good fortune as he climbed aboard the boat and it set off down the river.

Everyone on board took his turn at the oars, but as the youngest and fittest of the passengers, Ben noted that he was spending more time at the oars than anyone else. Finally, well after the sun had gone down and darkness had enveloped the river, several of the people aboard questioned whether they had rowed right past Philadelphia. They decided to make their way to the riverbank and wait there until sunrise to see where they really were. Ben slept the night on the ground beside a meager fire.

At dawn the others decided they had not passed Philadelphia after all, so everyone climbed back aboard the boat. In a little over an hour, they arrived at their destination.

As Ben walked up from the dock at the bottom of Market Street, the first thing he noticed about Philadelphia was how neat and orderly it was. The city had been laid out about forty years before by its founder, William Penn, using a grid pattern. It had none of the twisting, narrow streets that were the hallmark of Boston. Ben was soon noticing a lot of other differences from Boston. For one, his money seemed to go a lot further in Philadelphia. When he went to a local bakery to buy a loaf of bread, he found he could buy three loaves for the money he would pay for one loaf in Boston. And the people of Philadelphia seemed happier and more relaxed than the residents of Boston, except for one girl who stood at the door of a house and scowled at Ben as he went by. Ben felt his face turning red.

The girl was about his age and was dressed as a proper young lady. Ben glanced down at himself. His clothes were dirty, his pockets were stuffed with spare sets of socks and underwear, and he carried a loaf of bread under each arm as he hungrily devoured the third one.

Acutely aware of his appearance, Ben walked back to the dock and shared the two remaining loaves of bread with fellow passengers from the boat. It was Sunday morning, and not long afterward he spotted a surge of people headed for church. He followed them and soon found himself sitting in a Quaker meeting house. The service was unlike anything he had ever experienced in Boston. The members of the congregation sat quietly in their seats, either praying silently or meditating. Ben tried to copy them, but as soon as he closed his eyes, he fell asleep. He was astonished when an old man gently woke him at the end of the meeting. Ben felt embarrassed, but the Quakers around him spoke kindly and invited him to meet with them the following Sunday.

After the church service, Ben made his way back to the riverfront, where he struck up a conversation with a boy about his age. Ben asked the boy about the best place to find lodging in Philadelphia, and the boy led him to the Crooked Billet on King Street, beside the river. Ben rented a room and ate a hearty lunch. After lunch he slept all afternoon, and when the innkeeper woke him for dinner, Ben got up and ate another big meal and went straight back to bed.

The following morning Ben awoke fresh and alert. As the sun came up across the Delaware River and wrapped Philadelphia in a golden hue, Ben set out to find Andrew Bradford. He did not have a bath or breakfast before he left the Crooked Billet, as he was down to his last few pennies.

When Ben finally located Andrew Bradford's print shop, he was surprised to find someone he knew there—William Bradford. William had ridden a horse from New York to Philadelphia to visit his son. Ben was relieved when the two men asked him to join them for breakfast. He could easily have eaten twice as much as William and Andrew served him, but he did not want to appear too hungry.

Ben's heart sank when he heard that Andrew had already hired a new printer to take the place of the man who had recently died. However, William offered Ben some hope when he pointed out that a second printer had just set up shop in Philadelphia and offered to introduce Ben to him.

This second print shop belonged to Samuel Keimer, a small, bowlegged man with a long beard. Ben could not believe how disorganized and poorly stocked the shop was. There was only one typeface in which to set the type, and it was so worn that it was difficult to tell an *a* from an *o*. Rolls of paper were stacked up against the walls and under windows, where they would get damp and spoil. Ben marveled that anything got printed in the place at all. Still, he gratefully accepted the part-time job Samuel offered him.

Samuel recommended that Ben inquire about lodging at the house next door, as he thought that

Mr. and Mrs. Read, who lived there, were looking for a boarder. When Ben walked outside, he realized that the Reads' house was the place where the girl had stood at the door and scowled at him the day before. Ben knocked on the door, though his stomach was in knots at the thought of the rude girl possibly opening it. Instead he found himself talking to a plump woman, who offered him a place to live and the pleasure of meeting the spirited daughter of the house, Debby Read.

A week later, as Ben sat at the table eating Mrs. Read's venison stew and buns, it was hard for him to fathom how much his life had changed. He had gone from living in Boston under his brother's thumb to a job in Philadelphia, where no one knew anything about his family or his past except that he was a printer.

During that week, however, Ben had received a letter from one of his brothers-in-law, Robert Homes. Robert was a ship's captain who had heard through the grapevine that Ben was in Philadelphia. He wrote and asked Ben to make contact with his father and brother James. But Ben had no intention of doing so and wrote back a long letter to Robert, explaining to him how perfectly happy he was in Philadelphia and asking him not to tell the rest of his family of his whereabouts.

Ben did not know it, but that letter would change the course of his life and take him thousands of miles away.

Chapter 5

An Up-and-Coming Young Man

Samuel Keimer was in his late thirties, and he had many strange habits, all of which Ben felt it best not to comment on. He wore his beard long, never took a bath, and was very strict about not working on the Sabbath, though he never attended church. As far as Ben could tell, Samuel did not seem the least concerned that his printing press was in terrible shape or about the poor quality of pages that the rundown contraption produced. Still, Ben was grateful to have a job with a regular wage, and soon he was able to buy himself a silver watch on a chain, something he would not have been able to afford for years to come had he remained an apprentice for his brother in Boston.

One of the things that Ben loved most about being a printer was getting to meet many learned and interesting customers. One day, about two months after his arrival in Philadelphia, Ben heard a commotion outside the print shop. He turned to Samuel, and then they both looked out the window as the governor of Pennsylvania, William Keith, walked up.

"I think he's coming in!" Samuel exclaimed. "I do hope so. I've been trying to become the official printer of the colony for over a year now. Surely that's what the governor has come to talk to me about. Move over, Ben, I want to open the door myself."

Ben stood aside as Samuel pulled back the door and Governor Keith stepped inside.

Samuel bowed, and the governor nodded his head slightly, then turned toward Ben.

"So you must be the young Ben Franklin I've heard so much about," he said.

Ben stared at the governor, his mind whirling. Yes, his name was Ben Franklin, but he had no idea what he could have done to bring himself to the attention of the governor of Pennsylvania.

"Come, come," the governor said as he clapped Ben on the shoulder. He turned to Samuel. "I should like to borrow this young man for an hour or so. I trust that is not a problem to you?"

"No sir, not at all," Samuel replied, as he shot Ben an angry glance.

"Come along then, lad," the governor said. "I have a colonel from Delaware waiting at the tavern down the road for me. I fancy you could do with something to eat, eh?"

"Of course," Ben mumbled as he reached for his coat. He did not dare look at Samuel again. He knew that Samuel would be looking for answers as to why the governor was visiting him, and Ben did not have the slightest idea.

As the two men walked toward the tavern, the governor explained himself. "I am acquainted with your brother-in-law Captain Robert Homes," he began. "I was in Delaware when Robert's ship sailed in to winter over. I went to visit him, and just as I arrived, he happened to get a letter from you. He handed it to me to read, and I must say, I found it nearly impossible to imagine that it had been penned by a seventeen-year-old boy. The prose was perfect, the language crisp and to the point."

Ben felt himself blush. It was hard to hear such compliments, even though he had spent hundreds of hours teaching himself to write well.

Governor Keith nodded to a crowd who had gathered outside the tavern before continuing. "I was even more surprised, and I must say, delighted, when Robert informed me you had moved to Philadelphia and that you were a printer. I am sure you have had ample time to assess the dismal state of printing in the colony. There are only two print-shop owners, neither of whom I wish to award the government printing contract. One is too sloppy, and the other too slow."

By now Ben and the governor had entered the tavern and were shown to a private room to the left. Waiting there was Colonel French. Once formal introductions were made and the wine had started to flow, Governor Keith continued his conversation with Ben.

"The point is, young man, I have come to make you an offer. Set yourself up as an independent printer here, and I will guarantee you all the government printing jobs for Pennsylvania and Delaware, which I'm sure you are aware I also govern."

Ben felt that his eyes must be the size of the pewter plates on the table. He could hardly believe it. The most powerful man in the colony, perhaps in all of the colonies, was offering to be his patron.

"I don't know what to say," Ben finally mumbled.

"There's not much to say, really," chuckled Governor Keith. "Your brother-in-law tells me that you are an ambitious and capable young man. The question is not whether you will become my printer but how. Do you have any money to put toward starting yourself in business?"

Ben fingered the silver watch in his pocket; it represented all the wealth he had.

"No," he replied. "I came here with nothing, and I have not yet managed to save anything."

"No matter," the governor said, slicing another piece of thick, brown bread. "I supposed that would be the case. How about your father? Does he know a good business opportunity when he sees one?"

"It's possible," Ben replied, trying not to look disappointed. The last thing he wanted to do right then was to ask his father for a loan. But what if a loan was the only thing that stood between him and success?

Governor Keith talked on for several minutes, explaining how it was essential that Ben get his father to loan him money. The governor even offered to write a letter to Ben's father, laying out the plan for a new print shop and describing the bright future that lay ahead for Ben.

The more Ben listened, the more enthusiastic he became. He even found himself questioning how any father could say no to such an opportunity. Before they had finished eating, Ben had promised to return to Boston as soon as the shipping lanes opened in the spring in an effort to secure money from his father.

When Ben returned to work, Samuel was waiting anxiously to hear what the governor wanted with his young employee. Not wanting to give too much away, Ben spoke in vague terms about how Governor Keith was a friend of his brother-in-law and that he had promised to check up on Ben.

Over the next several weeks, the governor invited Ben to his home to discuss details of their plan, but Ben made sure that Samuel did not find out about these visits.

The spring thaw finally arrived, but it was not until late April 1724 that ships were once again making their way up and down the Delaware River and plying the East Coast sea routes. Ben took leave from work and booked passage on a ship back to Boston. The voyage was much less harrowing than his trip to Philadelphia, though the ship did scrape its bottom on a shoal in Delaware Bay. It sprang a leak, but rather than stop for repairs, the ship's captain decided to sail on, using the passengers as free labor to man the pumps. Ben did not mind the physical effort; it kept him warm and occupied his mind. But the closer he got to Boston, the more doubts he had about his plan.

Finally the ship sailed into Boston harbor and docked. The city had not changed much in the seven months Ben had been gone, though everything seemed more drab and restrictive compared to Philadelphia. Ben headed straight for the Franklin home on the corner of Union and Hanover Streets. He could feel his heart pounding as he stood at the door. Should he knock or go straight in? Was he a welcome family member or a prodigal son? There was only one way to find out, Ben decided as he opened the door. His father looked up and then rushed to greet him.

"We did not know whether you were dead or alive, and we did not know where to look for you," Josiah Franklin said. "How good it is to see you again, son."

Ben's mother could not contain her joy when she saw him. She threw her arms around him and hugged him as tears streamed down her face. Everyone, it seemed, was glad to see Ben safe and well—everyone, that is, except James. When Ben went to the print shop to see his brother, James barely acknowledged his presence and soon skulked off to his office. The two apprentices James had hired to replace Ben, however, were very excited to see him and fired off questions at him about Philadelphia and the job opportunities for printers there. Ben puffed out his chest as he answered, hoping the lads would notice his new suit of clothes and the watch chain that dangled from his pocket.

After several days of reacquainting himself with Boston and his family, Ben broached the subject of a loan with his father. He told him about meeting Governor Keith and his patronage, and how the governor intended for Ben to become the government printer for Pennsylvania, pointing out what a lucrative position this would eventually be.

Josiah Franklin listened quietly, but he was unmoved by Ben's passionate presentation. He asked Ben probing questions, including what sort of man would expect an eighteen-year-old to take such a loan on his young shoulders? Ben had no answer, and as the conversation continued, he knew he was not going to get any money from his father. He had to admit that deep in his heart he never thought he would.

Although Ben did not get what he wanted on his trip to Boston, some good had come out of it. His family, with the exception of James, had been glad to see him again, and before Ben left, his father had promised to lend him some money to get a business started when he turned twenty-one. Another good outcome of his trip to Boston was that his old friend John Collins had decided to move to Philadelphia. John had started out a week before for New York, where he would meet up with Ben.

As Ben boarded the sloop that would carry him to New York, he looked forward to spending a few days reading through John's library, which had been entrusted to him for the journey.

Ben did not know it until the ship was under way, but on board was a very important man, William Burnett, the governor of New York and New Jersey. When one of the sailors spotted Ben on deck reading a book, he informed the governor that there was another book lover aboard. The governor asked that Ben be brought to his cabin. Ben and the governor shared a love of books and spent many happy hours together discussing their favorite authors. For the second time in less than six months, Ben found himself on friendly terms with a powerful man.

Ben's happiness soon faded, however, when he disembarked in New York. John was not waiting for him at the dock as arranged, and it took Ben an entire day to track him down. When he did, Ben was appalled. The John Collins he knew was smart, hardworking, and sober, but the John Collins he found in New York was the opposite. John kept a bottle of brandy at his side and talked endlessly about the bills he had run up all over town and how he had no intention of paying them.

Scarcely able to understand how someone could change so quickly, Ben decided the best thing to do was to get John out of New York as fast as he could. He paid John's debts, and the two of them were soon on their way to Philadelphia.

Things were no better once they arrived in Philadelphia. Most of the time John was too drunk to look for a job. He eventually did manage to sober up long enough to apply for a job tutoring two young boys in the West Indies. Ben was very relieved when John got the position and sailed away.

With John gone, Ben was able to concentrate on finding another way to make his new print shop a reality. He visited Governor Keith several times, and much to his delight, the governor explained that he would personally do whatever was necessary to get

Ben started. He urged Ben to draw up a list of the equipment and supplies he would need to set up a print shop and then suggested that Ben sail to London to buy them himself.

Ben could hardly believe this turn of events, especially when Governor Keith promised to take care of everything. The governor booked Ben a passage to England on the colony's annual official mail ship and offered to write letters of introduction and credit to every major printing supplier in London.

It seemed to Ben that everything in his life was clicking into place. Not only was he on his way to becoming the government printer for Pennsylvania; he also was falling in love with Debby Read, the daughter of his landlady and, ironically, the girl who had scowled at him on his arrival in Philadelphia, when he looked like a ragamuffin. Debby's father had died unexpectedly while Ben was away in Boston, and the tragedy had drawn Ben closer to the family, especially to Debby. Mrs. Read, however, made it clear to Ben that she thought sixteen-year-old Debby was too young to marry. She suggested that Ben should wait until he got back from London before they decided whether they wanted to marry.

This suited Ben fine, as he had many other things to organize. He had to prepare for his departure and make sure that Governor Keith had made all the arrangements for him once he reached England.

Everything went smoothly, and on November 5, 1724, Benjamin Franklin walked up the gangway that led to the mail ship. In his pocket was a love letter from Debby, and on board, safely in the hands of the captain, were all of the letters of introduction and credit that he would need to make his way in the "home country," as people in the American colonies referred to England.

As he stepped confidently aboard the *London Hope*, Ben smiled broadly. As Ben saw it, no ship was more aptly named. The future for him was as bright as the rising sun the ship sailed toward.

Chapter 6

"Water American"

Ben learned two things during the seven-week voyage from Philadelphia to London. The first thing he learned was that the Atlantic Ocean was a rough and dangerous stretch of water to negotiate, and the second was that no matter how much the ship pitched and rolled, he seldom felt sick. So while most of the other passengers groaned below deck in their bunks, Ben spent his time on deck or in the salon reading and talking with the few other passengers unaffected by seasickness. One of these passengers was a Quaker merchant named Thomas Denham. Thomas was an older man who enjoyed discussing books, and he soon invited Ben to spend hours at a time keeping him company.

The days at sea passed pleasantly enough for Ben, and when the *London Hope* turned her bow into the English Channel, the captain allowed Ben to sort through the official bag of mail to find the letters Governor Keith had promised to include. Ben sorted through the letters in the bag once, twice, and then a third time. He was stunned. Not one letter in the mailbag was addressed to him! Impossible as it seemed, Governor Keith had failed to send any letters of credit and introduction for printing equipment and paper suppliers in London.

Ben was still sitting in shocked silence when Thomas Denham approached him. "What's wrong?" he asked, standing over Ben.

Ben could scarcely put his thoughts into words. He lifted up a pile of letters. "The captain let me look for my letters of credit and introduction from Governor Keith," he said, his voice barely above a whisper, "and there is not one letter here with my name on it." He dropped the letters back into the mailbag. "What could have happened? I am going to London on behalf of the governor to buy equipment and supplies. Why aren't the letters I need here?"

Thomas put his hand on Ben's shoulder. "You came all this way on the say-so of Governor Keith?" he asked. Ben could hear the incredulity in his voice.

"Yes," Ben replied. "He promised to set me up in business when I returned, and he said I could use his credit to get what I needed in London."

Suddenly Thomas burst out laughing. "I think you have been had, lad. It's common enough knowledge: Governor Keith has no credit to offer you. The man has more schemes in a week than could be realized in a lifetime."

Ben buried his face in his hands. "You mean I am going to be alone in London without any way to buy what I need."

"That's the short of it," Thomas replied. "Though at least you have a trade. You do have your papers with you, don't you?"

"Yes," Ben said. "I do have them, but I never thought I would have to use them to get work in London."

A day later the full impact of Governor Keith's oversight hit Ben. London, with its six hundred thousand inhabitants, was by far the biggest and the most confusing city Ben had ever seen. Sheep and cows were herded down the streets, and the River Thames was alive with cargo-laden ships. The Great Fire of London had leveled much of the city nearly sixty years before, and many new buildings and squares were still under construction.

Ben felt overwhelmed in this city, whose population was a hundred times greater than that of Boston, where he had grown up. To make matters worse, it was Christmas Day, and everyone seemed to have somewhere to go, except for him.

The only good thing about his first day in London was that Ben discovered that there were many print shops in the city. It was traditional in the printing trade for any printer to be given one day's work if he asked for it, and Ben immediately found a printer and claimed his right. That gave him enough money to find lodging for the night, and he worked at a different print shop the following day.

Within a week Ben had a steady job working for Samuel Palmer in Bartholomew Close. But setting row upon row of type was a long way from purchasing a fine printing press and stock of paper, as he had come to London to do,.and Ben fought the urge to sink into depression.

Ben's nineteenth birthday came and went without event. By then Ben had become known as the "Water American." This was because he preferred to drink water, while the other printers at the print shop—in fact, at all the shops in London—downed huge quantities of alcohol during the course of a workday. They drank a pint of beer before breakfast, another one with breakfast, more at midmorning, midday, and midafternoon, and they topped it off with another pint or two when work was over. So many of them spent Sunday in a drunken stupor that Monday was the most popular "sick day" of the week.

Being sober day in and day out gave Ben an advantage at work, especially when it came to the exacting task of setting type. Within several weeks Ben was being given the most difficult pages to typeset, and he earned a good wage for his labor. It wasn't long before he discovered the delights of London, including scores of theaters and bookstores to spend his money in.

By summer Ben found that he had become somewhat of a celebrity in the city. This was because of a skill he had taken for granted all his life—his ability to swim. While being a good swimmer was rare among people in New England, in

London it was considered a near miraculous talent. Once people learned that Ben could swim, they begged for demonstrations.

One day, after a visit to Chelsea, Ben was rowing home with several friends when they urged him to demonstrate his swimming ability. Ben stripped off his clothes and dived into the frigid water of the River Thames and began swimming behind the boat. First he swam overarm, then he switched to breaststroke, and finally to backstroke, before switching back to overarm. Ben watched in delight the astonished look on his friends' faces as they watched him in the water. "You look like you were born in the water," one of them called out. With that, Ben took a deep breath and swam even harder. He also noticed that people along the banks of the river stopped to watch. After swimming for three miles, Ben clambered back into the boat and let his friends row him the rest of the way home. Soon afterward two of his coworkers from the print shop asked Ben to teach them to swim, which he gladly did.

When word of Ben's prowess in the water reached Sir William Wyndham, he sent for Ben. Sir William explained that two of his sons were about to embark upon a long sea voyage, and he offered to pay Ben a generous fee if he would teach them to swim. Ben was unable to get the time off work he needed to teach the two boys to swim before they departed. However, he decided that if all else failed, he could probably make a good living in London teaching the sons of the well-to-do how to swim.

Time passed quickly in London, and Ben found that he was soon spending all his spare money on buying books and seeing plays. However, he realized that he would never get ahead if he kept spending all his money in this way, and so he decided it was time for him to return to Pennsylvania. The big question became how to afford the ten pounds a passage back across the Atlantic Ocean would cost.

It was a question that was answered in an unexpected manner. Thomas Denham, the Quaker merchant Ben had befriended on the voyage over, had bought half-shares in a ship and was preparing to set sail for Pennsylvania with a cargo of English goods. Thomas offered Ben free passage to the colony on the ship as well as a job as his assistant when they reached Philadelphia.

Ben gladly accepted the offer and set sail from London aboard the *Berkshire* in late July 1726. The ship sailed down the Thames and anchored overnight at Gravesend. However, that was the fastest progress the vessel made for the next twenty days. Strong easterly winds kept pushing the *Berkshire* back toward the coast, affording Ben a close-up view of the many coves and harbors along the English coastline before the ship finally made it out into the open sea.

On the journey back across the Atlantic, many of the passengers aboard the ship passed the time playing checkers and cards. During one of these card games, a Dutch passenger sitting next to Ben accused an Englishman of cheating. Tension quickly filled the room as the Dutchman demanded his bet back. The Englishman became indignant and refused to pay it. Ben waited quietly to see what would happen next. The captain was summoned, and he decided to hold an informal court hearing on the matter. Everyone sat around in the salon as several passengers were called to testify. After hearing the evidence, the captain found the Englishman guilty of cheating and fined him two bottles of brandy to be paid to the Dutchman. But the Englishman refused to pay the fine. So the captain ordered a sailor to hang him from the mainmast, not to kill him but to make him decide to pay the fine. Ben watched as the man was hoisted up and dangled several feet off the deck.

After about fifteen minutes, the man's face began to turn black, and the captain ordered the man cut down. Still, the man refused to pay his fine, and so he was ordered to remain in his cabin for the rest of the voyage. Finally, after two days of isolation, the Englishman paid the fine and rejoined the other passengers. Ben was fascinated by the situation, and he wrote in his journal:

> Man is a sociable being, and it is for aught I know one of the worst of punishments to be excluded from society. I have read abundance of fine things on the subject of solitude, and I know 'tis a common boast in the mouths of those that affect to be thought wise, that they are never less alone than when alone. I acknowledge solitude an agreeable

refreshment to a busy mind; but were these thinking people obliged to be always alone, I am apt to think they would quickly find their very being insupportable to them.

It was not only the behavior of his fellow passengers that fascinated Ben, who made many other observations on the journey back across the Atlantic Ocean. Ben watched sharks and dolphins as they trailed the ship, making notes on their movements. He watched a partial eclipse of the sun and became intrigued with the long tendrils of kelp that floated on the surface of the water. Ben decided to do an experiment with the kelp. He observed that many small crabs lived among the kelp, and he wondered if the crabs were a kind of fruit of the kelp, emerging from it to be sustained by it. To test his theory he scooped up some kelp without any crabs on it and placed it in a bucket of seawater on deck. Over the next several days, he closely watched the kelp, hoping to see the crabs emerge from it. When no crabs emerged, Ben decided that his theory was wrong and that the crabs must come from someplace other than the kelp itself.

On the journey Ben also thought a lot about why he had gone to England in the first place and how he could be wiser in the future. By the time the *Berkshire* approached the coastline of North America, he had written down four principles of conduct that would guide his behavior once he arrived back in Philadelphia:

1. It is necessary for me to be extremely frugal for some time, till I have paid what I owe.

2. To endeavor to speak truth in every instance; to give nobody expectations that are not likely to be answered, but aim at sincerity in every word and action—the most amiable excellence in a rational being.

3. To apply myself industriously to whatever business I take in hand, and not divert my mind from my business by any foolish project of growing suddenly rich; for industry and patience are the surest means of plenty.

4. I resolve to speak ill of no man whatever, not even in a matter of truth; but rather by some means excuse the faults I hear charged upon others, and upon proper occasion speak all the good I know of every body.

As he read and reread these points, Ben realized that he had given Debby Read and her mother the expectation that he would write regularly while he was away and would return to marry Debby. In reality Ben had written only once, and he had no idea how he felt about Debby after two years. All he could do was hope that the Reads would be forgiving and that perhaps he and Debby could take up where they left off.

Finally, on October 9, 1726, Cape Henlopen, at the mouth of Delaware Bay, came into view on the horizon. Several days later Ben once again set foot in Philadelphia. He was home. And that is what it truly felt like to him. Although he had been born and raised in Boston and had just spent two years in England, Philadelphia was the place he thought of as home, and it was good to be back.

Chapter 7

Skill and Industry

Many things had changed in Pennsylvania in the nearly two years Ben had been away. Sir William Keith was no longer the governor of the colony, and Philadelphia was thriving. In fact, it was fast taking over from Boston as the largest city in the colonies.

Ben loved walking around the city, looking at the new stores and businesses that had opened while he was away and reacquainting himself with his old friends, that is, except for Debby Read. Word had quickly reached Ben on his arrival in Philadelphia that Debby had given up hope of his ever returning to the colony to marry her, and she had gone ahead and married a potter named John Rogers. Although Ben did not know the details of the marriage, he understood that it was not a happy one and that John was rumored to have another wife in England. All of this made Ben feel ashamed. He wished he had written to Debby more regularly while in England, but he had not, and now there seemed little he could do to rectify the situation.

To take his mind off Debby, Ben threw himself into helping Thomas Denham open a general merchant store on Front Street. Thomas, who had no sons of his own, insisted on teaching Ben all he knew about being a merchant. Soon Ben was doing the bookkeeping for the store, along with selling and ordering new merchandise from London. The future looked bright, especially when Thomas hinted that Ben would one day inherit everything he owned.

Fate intervened once again, however, turning the course of Ben's life. In April 1727, six months after he and Ben had returned to Philadelphia, Thomas became ill and died. Since he had not recorded his intentions toward Ben in a written will, his estate was taken over by trustees, and Ben was once more without a job. All of this stunned Ben, who by now had become very aware of just how precarious promises of patronage could be. He was faced with the immediate task of finding work for himself.

Ben investigated setting himself up as a merchant but soon realized that it took the right connections to begin something that ambitious, and he did not have such connections. So he turned back to the thing he knew best—printing. However, since he had saved no money in the short time he had been back in the colony, he did not have the option of starting his own business. Instead he went cap in hand to Samuel Keimer and asked for his old job back. Ben was surprised to learn that Samuel's business was booming. Samuel now employed five men in his printing shop—three bonded laborers and two men on hourly wages. Samuel explained to Ben that he now wanted to open a stationery store and offered to pay Ben fifty pounds a year to train the five men to be competent printers.

Ben took the job, but it did not take him long to figure out what Samuel was up to. He overheard Samuel telling someone that he intended to fire Ben as soon as Ben had passed on all his printing knowledge to the cheaper workers. With this in mind, Ben decided to take advantage of the situation himself. He used his spare time and Samuel's equipment to experiment with making various types of cast letters so that he would not have to continually send to England for replacements. He also perfected engraving and ink making, the rudiments of which he had learned while in London. However, he was careful not to teach these skills to the others so that he would have an edge when Samuel fired him.

Over the weeks, tensions between Ben and Samuel grew, until one day they finally boiled over. A disturbance had erupted outside the courthouse, just up the street from the print shop. Ben walked over to the window to investigate what was going on. It was then that Samuel exploded, chastising Ben for neglecting his work. Ben was stung by his boss's comments, and he shot back an insult at Samuel. The argument got louder and more ugly, until Samuel started cursing and telling Ben that he wanted to fire him.

"That will not be necessary," Ben snapped. "I quit!" And with that he turned, picked up his hat and coat, and walked out of the print shop.

It had been a hotheaded thing to do, Ben had to admit, as he strolled back to his boardinghouse in midafternoon. But he refused to entertain the idea of going back to Samuel and apologizing. He told himself that something else would turn up, and it did. That night, Hugh Meredith paid him a visit. Hugh was one of the bonded laborers whom Ben had been training. Hugh showed a lot of promise as a printer. He explained to Ben that he had just talked with his father, who was willing to finance the two of them in a printing business when the duration of Hugh's employment bond to Samuel was over.

The next evening, Ben met with Hugh's father, who told Ben that he wanted to finance him into his own print shop for two reasons. First, he said that Ben was probably the finest printer in the colony. And second, he was particularly impressed with Ben's clean lifestyle and the effect it had had on Hugh. He explained that since Hugh had been working with Ben, he had stopped drinking alcoholic spirits and had for the first time ever taken pride in his work.

The offer excited Ben, but he still had to find a way to survive for the next several months while Hugh finished his employment bond at the print shop. Then a letter arrived from Samuel, saying he was sorry for the argument and that two men ought not to part company under such circumstances. He even offered Ben his job back. Ben was surprised by Samuel's change of heart and accepted the offer of his old job back—for the present time, anyway.

Ben soon learned why his employer had apologized so readily. Samuel had just won a contract to print new money for New Jersey. Not only was it a big job, but it was very precise work that needed to be carried out by someone with a good knowledge of engraving. Ben knew that he was the only printer in Pennsylvania and New Jersey who could do the work.

Soon Ben was carving intricate designs for the new banknotes onto copper plates that would be used in the printing process. Officials in New Jersey were so impressed with the quality of the banknotes Ben had produced that they extended Samuel's contract to print money for the colony.

Meanwhile Ben did not lose sight of the opportunity that awaited him when Hugh Meredith's bond was up in the spring of 1728, and Ben secretly prepared himself to begin his own business. He sent to England for the typefaces and printing presses he would need to set up the new print shop.

As he worked away printing new banknotes for New Jersey, Ben thought about other things. Oddly, his mind turned to growing up in Boston and, in particular, to the old Puritan patriarch Cotton Mather. For all his narrow ways, Cotton Mather had started some wonderful institutions in

Boston. One that had always impressed Ben was the church discussion groups he oversaw. In these groups men talked about Scripture and read sermons together. They did something else in these groups too: they supported one another in their attempts to better themselves. Ben found himself desperately wanting to belong to such a group, though one without the emphasis on religion. He wanted to be part of a community of like-minded friends who could help one another to establish themselves in town. Since no such group existed in Philadelphia, Ben decided to start one.

Ben decided to call the new group the Junto Club, though it was also known as the Club of the Leather Aprons because most of the men who attended were tradesmen, such as silversmiths, shoemakers, glaziers, ironworkers, and carpenters. The group got together on a regular basis to discuss history, morality, poetry, physics, travel, mechanics, and the arts. In addition, the members of the group spent a lot of time encouraging one another in various business opportunities.

The Junto Club gave Ben just the right kind of support he needed to launch the printing venture in the spring of 1728. Ben and Hugh rented a house on Market Street to serve as their print shop, and to help pay the bills, they sublet the upstairs to a young married couple. Even though Hugh's father was backing them financially, money was still extremely tight. To make matters worse, there was little printed money in circulation in Philadelphia, so to get printing jobs, Ben was forced to accept payment for jobs in everything from venison to sail-cloth and cabbages. To keep their costs down, Ben and Hugh ran errands and swept the floors themselves instead of hiring a boy to do it. Ben reminded himself that humility was one of the virtues that he had decided to live by, and he strived to be content taking care of all the lowly jobs of a struggling business owner.

Throughout this time, Ben planned his future. One of the things he decided he needed to establish was his own newspaper to rival the *American Mercury*, which was produced by Andrew Bradford, the other printer in town. However, Samuel Keimer got wind of Ben's plan and hastily started his own newspaper, which he named *The Universal Instructor in All Arts and Sciences: and Pennsylvania Gazette.*

At first Ben was frustrated by this turn of events, but he soon came to see it as a blessing. Samuel's newspaper was proving to be too much for him and his staff to handle, and within months Samuel was knocking on Ben's door, asking if he would like to buy out the paper.

At the same time, Hugh's father had fallen on hard times financially and announced that he would no longer be able to bankroll Ben and Hugh in their print-shop venture. Soon, however, a solution presented itself. Two of Ben's friends from the Junto Club offered to lend Ben enough money to buy out Hugh's interest in the print shop and to purchase Samuel's newspaper.

Ben jumped at the opportunity, and within weeks he was the sole owner of a print shop and a newspaper. Suddenly he felt like everything was going his way. He was certain that by using his skill and industry he could finally get ahead in the printing world.

The first thing he did after purchasing the newspaper was to shorten its name to the *Pennsylvania Gazette*. Then he set to work. He did almost everything himself, from wheelbarrowing loads of paper from the docks to the print shop to writing fake letters to the editor and then answering them himself.

The business grew steadily, and Ben soon expanded it to sell stationery, business and legal forms, and religious books that he imported from England.

Now that Ben was confident that he could make a good living in his new venture, he turned his attention to personal matters: he decided that he needed a wife. This future wife would need to be someone who would love both a husband and a baby—the year before, a son had been born to Ben in a relationship that ended quickly. Ben had handled it as best he could by raising the baby himself.

As Ben thought about a wife, he found his thoughts turning once again to Debby Read Rogers. Ben had heard from mutual friends that her husband had abandoned her and gone to the Caribbean to seek his fortune, or perhaps another wife.

Ben visited Debby's house and found that Mrs. Read blamed herself and not him for her daughter's predicament. Mrs. Read admitted to Ben that she had urged Debby to give up on waiting for Ben and to settle for John's marriage proposal.

Despite the fact that John had deserted his wife, Debby had no way to legally free herself from him. Desertion was no grounds for divorce in Pennsylvania. If Ben and Debby married and John returned to claim his wife, both Ben and Debby would be sentenced to thirty-nine lashes with a whip in the public square, followed by life in jail.

It was quite a dilemma. Ben still loved Debby, and she loved him. After a lot of soul searching, they decided it would be safest for them to become husband and wife under common law, which they did publicly on September 1, 1730.

Debby and Ben moved into the rooms above the printing shop on Market Street, and a week later Ben's newborn baby, whom Ben had named William, joined them. Ben and Debby set about making a home for themselves and William Franklin. Their future seemed predictable and secure, and, indeed, Ben seemed able to successfully pursue whatever his talented mind could think of.

An Up-and-Coming Businessman

A year later Ben Franklin was gratified to note that his new family was prospering. He worked hard at his printing business, and his efforts were paying off. With the money he earned, he was easily able to support his family. Debby was proving to be a great asset too, not only in the home but also in the business. She was a hard worker, and although she made many spelling mistakes, she was able to read and write enough to take over keeping the accounts for the *Pennsylvania Gazette* as well as help with counting and collating the newspaper. Debby's mother, Sarah, moved in with the family, and she helped take care of William and expand the stationery shop. Sarah had made and sold various skin creams for many years, and these found their way onto the shelves of the shop, as did bolts of fabric and lace and boxes of tea from England, along with two items imported from Boston: Ben's mother's soap and his father's candles. The shop prospered from the outset, allowing Ben to set aside money to print entire books as well as pamphlets and the newspaper.

In 1731 most books in the American colonies came from London and were housed almost entirely in private libraries belonging to either wealthy families or churches. But Ben decided it was time for a change. He proposed to the members of the Junto Club that they establish a circulating library that would lend books to the general public to read and further their education. It was a new idea; no library like that existed in the American colonies. However, the members of the club warmed to the idea, and soon Ben was drafting a charter for what would be known as the Library Company of Philadelphia. According to the charter, the initial fee for joining the library was forty shillings, with an annual subscription fee of ten shillings. Those who subscribed to the library could then borrow one book at a time from the library to take home and read, though any member of the general public could peruse the books on the library shelves. It was agreed that when fifty initial subscriptions had been collected, the library would be established.

With the charter in place, it fell to twenty-five-year-old Ben Franklin to begin collecting the initial subscriptions. At the start this proved more difficult than he had anticipated, and he soon learned why. Ben had presented the idea as his and had asked the people to trust him with their forty shillings. But he realized that this made people suspicious of his motives. They wondered exactly what was in it for Ben. What was he getting out of the plan? So Ben changed his approach. Instead of presenting it as *his* idea, he began presenting the Library Company as a scheme put together by a number of leading citizens in the community who had enlisted Ben to represent them and collect the money. This new approach worked much better, and soon Ben had collected the initial fifty subscriptions.

Now it was time to purchase the books for the new library. Ben made a list of those volumes that he thought a well-stocked library should have on its shelves, and then he visited James Logan. James had been the personal assistant to William Penn, the founder of Pennsylvania, and was reputed to be the most educated man in the colony. He knew Latin, Greek, Hebrew, French, and Italian. He also had a deep understanding of mathematics and science. James was the acting governor of the colony, and Ben wanted him to suggest books that a well-educated and well-rounded person ought to read.

James also suggested that Ben seek the approval of Thomas Penn, William Penn's younger son, who had inherited the colony from his father. Thomas Penn had a reputation for being rude and uncooperative, so Ben was surprised when he agreed to be the patron of the Library Company.

When the list of books was finally complete, it included volumes on a range of topics, including mathematics, philosophy, metaphysics, literature, poetry, natural science, and even practical subjects such as gardening. Ben sent the list off to London, where the books were ordered. Before long the books began arriving. Ben read every one of them before they were stacked on the shelves. Initially the library was open for an hour on Wednesday afternoons and for six hours on Saturdays, and soon people were streaming through its doors to borrow books. Nothing could have pleased Ben more. He thought of how Matthew Adams had opened his family's library to Ben as a boy back in Boston and of the difference that that gesture had made in his life. He believed that books had the power to change the life of everyone who read them.

Setting up the library and arranging patronage for it made Ben one of the most prominent men in Philadelphia, and many doors were opened to him.

In October 1732 the Franklin household was enlarged when Debby gave birth to a baby boy. She and Ben named him Francis Folger Franklin. Francis was a healthy child who thrived from the start.

Ben was very happy, with everything in his life going smoothly. The assembly, the governing body of the colony, which was under the control of Thomas Penn, chose Ben's print shop to print the colony's new banknotes and other official papers. By now Ben employed several competent journeymen, and he used some of the money he received from the government contract to set them up in print shops in other colonies. The first printer, Thomas Whitmarsh, went to South Carolina, where he immediately became the official printer of that colony. Ben had three major advantages in this arrangement. First, he got a share of any profits the print shops made. Second, he got to buy larger quantities of paper, which allowed him to negotiate larger discounts than normal. Third, the printers he partnered with shared with him news and information from their colonies, much of which found its way into the pages of the *Pennsylvania Gazette.* The newspaper was soon recognized as the leading paper in North America.

Apart from posters, the newspaper was the only way to get a message out to the general public. As a result, the *Gazette* carried all sorts of announcements and advertisements. When a ship arrived in port, the paper printed notices about the cargo on board. Thomas Chew, the merchant located down the street from Ben, advertised, "A considerable quantity of fresh drugs just imported from London are to be sold in large or small parcels." People were bought and sold through the newspaper too. One ad read, "A very likely Negro woman aged about thirty years who has lived in this city from her childhood and can wash and iron very well, cook victuals, sew, spin on the linen wheel, milk cows, and do all sorts of housework very well. She has a boy of about two years old, which is to go with her.... And also another very likely boy aged about six years who is the son of the abovesaid woman. He will be sold with his mother, or by himself, as the buyer pleases."

Ben also printed notices about runaway servants, including "a servant man named John Homer,

by trade a shoemaker, of short stature, pale com-
plexion, one of his feet hath been half cut off, and
three toes off the other. He had on a light double-
breasted coat with light-coloured buttons, and he
rode on a small dark bay horse."

Ben occasionally got himself into trouble for
printing something that angered people in the community. He always defended the right of a newspaper editor to present alternate views on a subject
in the hope of educating the public. Still, he was
careful to edit out those things that he knew could
be considered offensive. On one occasion, however,
as he was hurriedly compiling the latest issue of
the *Gazette,* he let slip through an advertisement
that created quite a stir. The ad announced the
imminent departure of a ship for Barbados in the
Caribbean. Tucked at the bottom were the words,
"No Sea Hens nor Black Gowns will be admitted on
any terms."

Both *sea hens* and *black gowns* were insulting
terms used to describe clergymen in the Anglican
Church. Within an hour of the paper's hitting the
streets, Ben was getting complaints for insulting
the clergymen. Ben apologized at the oversight,
though in his defense he pointed out that he had
never before heard of clergymen being referred to as
sea hens. This was enough to settle the issue for
many people, but for others it was not. So Ben
recited a fable to illustrate the situation in which he
found himself. He told of a father and son traveling
to market to sell their donkey. The old man rode on
the donkey while his son walked alongside. But

other travelers on the road criticized the father for this, telling him that he should be ashamed that his son had to walk while he rode. So the father pulled his son up behind him onto the donkey, and they rode on. The next travelers they met criticized them for unmercifully burdening down the donkey. So the father got off and walked along while his son rode. This time his son was criticized for riding while his father walked. So they decided to both walk and lead the donkey. This time they were criticized for being stupid, leading a perfectly good donkey along when they could be riding it. Finally, in frustration the father said to his son, "It grieves me much that I cannot please all of these people. Let's throw the donkey over the next bridge and be no more troubled with the animal."

Ben pointed out that if the father had followed through on this plan, people would have called him a fool for trying to please everyone. He wrote, "Therefore, though I have a temper almost as complying as his, I intend not to imitate him in this last particular. I consider the variety of humours among men, and despair of pleasing everybody, yet I shall not therefore leave off printing. I shall continue my business. I shall not burn my press and melt my letters."

In an "Apology for Printers," which Ben wrote and published in the *Pennsylvania Gazette*, he said, "Printers are educated in the belief that when men differ in opinion both sides ought equally to have the advantage of being heard by the public; and that when truth and error have fair play, the former is always an overmatch for the latter: Hence they cheerfully serve all contending writers that pay them well, without regarding on which side they are of the question in dispute."

The controversy finally blew over, and Ben's printing business grew in proportion to the size of the growing Pennsylvania colony. As more immigrants and goods flooded into the colony, Ben continued doing a brisk business in selling advertisements in the *Pennsylvania Gazette.*

With each weekly edition, the *Pennsylvania Gazette* became more popular, and Ben looked for other moneymaking projects. In the fall of 1732 he had decided to produce an almanac. Ben had learned that the leading almanac writer in the colonies sold between fifty thousand and sixty thousand copies a year, more than the total of all other books sold in the colonies. In fact, next to the Bible, almanacs were the most popular books in colonial homes. Almanacs were popular because they were part entertainment and part information. They contained such practical information as a calendar, a planting guide, a table of the phases of the moon and the tides, as well as recipes, games, fashion tips, and witty sayings.

Ben decided that he would not write the almanac under his own name but would instead use the made-up name of Richard Saunders. He had a lot of fun pretending to be Richard Saunders and thinking of a good reason why he would want to write an almanac. In the front page of the book, Ben included a letter from "Richard" explaining the stressful home situation that had led him to put so much effort into the publication.

> Courteous Reader, I might in this place attempt to gain thy favor by declaring that I write almanacks with no other view than the public good; but in this I should not be sincere, and men are nowadays too wise to be deceived by pretenses how specious so-ever. The plain truth of the matter is, I am excessive poor, and my wife, good woman, is, I tell her, excessive proud. She cannot bear, she says, to sit spinning in her shift of tow while I do nothing but gaze at the stars, and has threatened to burn all my books and rattling-traps (as she calls my instruments) if I do not make some profitable use of them for the good of my family. The printer has offered me some considerable share of the profits, and I have thus begun to comply with my Dame's desire.

Ben named his almanac *Poor Richard's Almanack*, and two years after the first edition of it appeared, the book was doing as well as Ben had hoped. The profits from his print shop, as well as from the print shops he had set up as partnerships in other colonies, earned Ben over two hundred pounds a year, making him a rich man. With this money Ben was able to buy several empty lots farther up Market Street, where he built a spacious new house for his family.

Both Ben's family and his business were prospering, and Ben looked around for a new project to tackle. He decided that he would find a way to improve Philadelphia.

Chapter 9

A Civic-Minded Man

When William Penn founded Philadelphia, he had planned it as a "green city," with lots of parks and open spaces. However, when he died, his sons abandoned this plan, and many of the common areas and parks had been sold off as house lots. This in turn made the city dirty, overcrowded, and difficult to get around quickly. In his campaign to correct some of these obvious problems, Ben Franklin decided to focus on improving what he saw as the most annoying thing about Philadelphia—its streets. Thanks to William Penn's foresight, the streets were broad and straight, but they were also unpaved. This meant that in spring, small streams gouged paths down them and the wheels of carriages and carts were bogged down in mud. In summer the streets were deeply rutted, and every horse and wagon kicked up billows of dust. Since Philadelphia's streets were no better or worse than the streets of other cities in the American colonies, no one but Ben appeared to imagine any prospect of improving them.

Ben thought long and hard about how to change the minds of his fellow citizens and get them to pay the money needed to pave their streets. He began convincing his closest friends at the Junto Club. Eventually they agreed that having paved streets was an interesting idea, but they doubted that Ben would be successful in raising the money. However, Ben had a plan. He wrote several letters complaining about the state of the streets in Philadelphia to the editor of the *Pennsylvania Gazette*, who, of course, was he. As editor, Ben responded to the letters, agreeing that the streets were indeed a nuisance and suggesting how pleasant it would be if they were less dusty and bumpy and how much the good citizens of Philadelphia deserved the best streets in the colonies. As Ben walked around town, he smiled when he overheard conversations about the possibility of paving the streets. His plan was working.

The next phase in his plan to improve the state of the streets was to develop a model street so that many people would have the opportunity of both seeing and trying out a paved road. He chose as his test case one of the streets that ran through the market. Ben used his own money to pave the street with stones. He then hired a man to sweep the street twice a week and remove all of the garbage and horse manure from in front of the houses and shops.

The results were amazing. Suddenly everyone was clamoring to have his street paved and his garbage collected. Ben struck quickly, drafting a bill to have the streets in the entire city paved. He even included a provision for a novel idea—street lighting. Even though adopting the bill would mean that each property owner in the city would have to pay taxes for the project, the bill passed the Pennsylvania Assembly, and the streets were paved.

Ben was delighted. Not only could he now ride around town in more comfort, but also he got great pleasure in knowing that he had inspired people to improve their city.

Encouraged by the success of the street paving, Ben looked around for another civic project. He decided to tackle an issue that had worried him ever since his visit to London: the possibility that Philadelphia could have a citywide fire.

On September 2, 1666, a huge fire had ravaged London. The fire had started in a bakery in Pudding Lane. It had been a particularly dry summer, and fanned by a strong breeze, the fire soon spread to surrounding buildings. At the end of three days, four-fifths of the city of London had been razed. When Ben arrived in London sixty years later, much of the city had been rebuilt, but many signs of the ferociousness of the fire were still visible. Ben had fretted about the havoc and destruction such a fire would cause in Philadelphia. So, using the same methods he had used to get the streets paved, he set about generating interest in the founding of a fire company. He started by presenting a paper on the subject to the Junto Club and followed it up with a series of letters to the editor of the *Pennsylvania Gazette*, which he wrote under the pseudonym A.A.

Writing as A.A., Ben described himself as an old man with lame hands who was afraid that his wooden house would catch on fire. If it did, he complained, he would not be strong enough to get himself out of the building in time, much less carry any of his goods to safety. "An ounce of prevention is worth a pound of cure," he wrote, and then he went on to outline a long list of things he thought the good people of Philadelphia should do to help him and others like him.

Among his list, A.A. urged the citizens of Philadelphia to take care when carrying hot embers from one hearth to another. "For," he wrote, "scraps of fire may fall into chinks and make no appearance till midnight; when your stairs being in flames, you may be forced (as I once was) to leap out of your windows and hazard your necks to avoid being oven-roasted."

A.A. also wanted the common practice of framing fireplaces with pinewood to be declared illegal, as the pine tar sometimes caught fire. He also suggested regulating bakeries and coopers' shops to make sure that their fireplaces were large enough to contain the fires that were lit in them every morning. Chimney sweeps also became an object of reform. A.A. wanted them to be licensed by the mayor and fined for any chimney that caught fire within two weeks of their cleaning it.

The letters in the *Gazette* and numerous conversations at the Junto Club on the subject of a fire company began to pay off. And just as with the street improvements, many people started talking about the dangers of fire and how a fire company would make them feel safer.

Ben viewed stirring up such public interest as his biggest civic achievement so far, but this was marred by a family tragedy in November 1736. Four-year-old Francis came down with smallpox and died within forty-eight hours. Ben and Debby were heartbroken, and even more so because Ben had intended to get his young son inoculated against the disease as soon as Francis had recovered from a cold. Now it was too late. Ben tried to placate his grief by hastening the formation of a fire company, and just a month after Francis's death, the Union Fire Company was incorporated.

The new fire company consisted of twenty-five members who each agreed to purchase two leather buckets for carrying water and four cloth bags for rescuing goods from a burning building. Any member who did not show up at a fire at a fellow member's home with his firefighting equipment was to be fined five shillings. The members also agreed to meet monthly to go over the policies of the Union Fire Company, though Ben shrewdly turned the meetings into social gatherings so that more men would want to join.

Sure enough, Ben's plan paid off, and soon other fire companies were springing up around the city.

Now that Philadelphia had fire companies, Ben turned his attention to the next troubling issue at hand, that of the police force. The city had no real police force, just a neighborhood watch system by which each household was supposed to produce an adult male to take his turn patrolling the streets at night. For a sum of six shillings a year, a substitute could be hired, but these hired men were often drunkards and nuisances.

As usual, Ben had a better idea. He lobbied to hire a full-time police force and pay for it by a tax on every citizen. Since rich citizens had more property to protect, he suggested that they pay a higher rate. As with his other schemes, the idea of a full-time police force caught on, and soon Philadelphia became one of the safest cities in the American colonies.

With all of this civic activity, it did not surprise Ben when he was elected to serve as the clerk of court. Ben's main job as the clerk of court was to keep an accurate record of everything that was said during debates and votes in the Pennsylvania Assembly. For the most part, Ben found this interesting, especially when the debates revolved around the role of Thomas Penn, the proprietor of the colony, and the members of the assembly, whose job it was to govern the everyday affairs of the colony under the governor. The assembly and Thomas Penn seemed to be engaged in a constant tug-of-war over the direction of the colony, with the governor stuck in the middle. The governor was appointed by Thomas Penn, who also told him what to do, but the assembly paid his salary. Ben often chuckled to himself as he observed the dilemma the governor faced. Did he side with the man who had appointed him and had the power to fire him or with the men who paid his wages?

For his part, Ben found that many of the politicians in the assembly recognized that he was an influential man in Pennsylvania, and in private conversations they began to ask him to support their plans and ideas in the *Pennsylvania Gazette*. Ben, however, prided himself on being his own man and decided to show these politicians and friends that they did not own him and that his influence could not be bought. To do this, Ben invited a number of influential people to dinner one evening. He asked Debby to set the table with their finest china and then instructed her to serve the guests only porridge and water. This, of course, shocked the dinner guests, who had come expecting a five-course dinner, not porridge and water. Ben ignored the strange looks he was getting from those around him and ate heartily. He told jokes and laughed uproariously during the one-course meal, and when they were done eating, he stood and addressed the guests.

"Gentlemen," he said, "I have brought you here tonight to demonstrate a point I wish each of you to remember. A man such as I, who can be content to eat porridge and drink water three times a day, has no need of the patronage or money any of you could offer me."

His point was well taken, and Ben soon noticed that fewer men were trying to win him over to their side of a debate with bribes or offering to involve him in secret deals.

In November 1737 Ben reflected back over the year since Francis had died. In many ways it had been a whirlwind of activity. In addition to his work at the *Gazette* and as the clerk of court, each Monday was taken up with running the library, Union Fire Company meetings, and other local affairs. Then each Friday evening Ben met with the Junto Club, and on his free evenings he set himself the task of learning French, Italian, Spanish, and Latin.

There were times, though, when Ben did feel the need to relax. On these occasions he turned to his bath. The Franklin home was the only one on the street with a bath, and Ben knew that many people thought he was strange for being so fond of it. But he believed that the human body should be clean and well-aired, and so he liked to soak in his bath for up to two hours at a time. (The bath had a lid over half of it to keep the heat in.) On most days, while taking his bath, Ben occupied himself creating magic squares. He would draw a grid of sixteen squares across and sixteen squares down and fit numbers into each square so that the sum of every row horizontally, vertically, and diagonally was the same. Sometimes it took many hours of working to get this right, but Ben enjoyed the mental exercise.

Ben loved being busy, and now, as he walked down the streets of Philadelphia, he could see the results of his labor everywhere he went. Men were paving new streets and installing streetlights, fire companies protected many houses, and the citizens could rest easier at night, knowing that they had a full-time police force protecting them.

As Ben thought about it, he realized that making other people's lives better gave him a tremendous sense of achievement. So when some members of the Junto Club suggested that he apply to become the postmaster of Pennsylvania, his mind buzzed with possibilities. He knew that he could reform the postal service to become the best in the colonies.

Besides wanting to reform the postal service, Ben was eager to become postmaster for another reason. The current postmaster was rival printer Andrew Bradford, and since the postmaster had total control over the mail service, Bradford had forbidden any of his mail carriers to deliver the *Pennsylvania Gazette*. Making matters even more unfair, Bradford's newspaper, the *American Mercury*, was delivered free to anyone in the colony who ordered it. Such favorable treatment infuriated Ben, who determined that it was time for a change.

To Ben's advantage, Bradford was so used to being postmaster that his accounting practices had become very sloppy. Eventually Thomas Penn became so frustrated at not receiving the proper postal taxes that he fired Bradford, creating the need to appoint a new postmaster.

Ben knew that Thomas Penn was not particularly enthusiastic about his having the job, because he had been critical of the Penns in the pages of the *Gazette*. But by now Ben had powerful friends in the assembly who lobbied on his behalf. Practicality was on Ben's side as well. The postmaster needed an office, which Ben already had, and a bookkeeper, a job that Debby had learned to do well.

Late in 1737 Ben Franklin was appointed postmaster, and he set to work right away. The first thing he did was to start circulating the *Pennsylvania Gazette* through the mail. As a result, the weekly number of copies of the paper printed jumped to two thousand. And although Andrew Bradford had banned the *Pennsylvania Gazette* from the mail, Ben did not do the same thing to his paper. Instead he allowed the postriders to carry both newspapers, trusting that the better paper would win the hearts and minds of the readers.

Ben also tackled the matter of payment for postage. Since the person receiving the mail, not the sender, paid the postage on it, there were often difficulties extracting money to pay for the postage. That was not the only problem. It was often difficult to track people down because addresses were vague, and the mail took so long to arrive that people had often moved from their previous addresses. To correct this problem, Ben came up with a novel idea. He printed in his newspaper the name of everyone who had uncollected mail. This served the double purpose of having more mail collected (and paid for) and making his newspaper more useful to people.

By 1738 things were running smoothly with the postal service. Debby now took care of the bookkeeping and post office business while Ben concentrated on the ever-growing demand for his printing services. By now Ben was the official printer for Delaware and New Jersey as well as for Pennsylvania, and *Poor Richard's Almanack* was growing more popular with each successive edition. In fact, things were going so well that Ben decided it was time to have his portrait painted. He had never before thought that he had enough money to spend on something so impractical as this, but now he decided the time had come. He engaged the services of a portrait painter, bought a new curled wig and ruffled shirt, and struck his most dignified pose. As he gazed at the portrait, he was proud that he was an English colonial gentleman. He had no way of predicting that he wouldn't always be proud to be English or be satisfied to be a colonial.

Chapter 10

Scientist and Inventor

Two years later Ben was still looking for ways to be useful. One of the things he began to focus on was the way homes were heated. Just about all of the houses in the American colonies were heated by an open fire in a fireplace, with a chimney running up through the roof. The chimneys belched smoke back into living rooms and kitchens, and it was nearly impossible to get an even temperature in a room with an open fire. People sitting close to the fire were too hot, while those sitting away from it were too cold. Moreover, open fireplaces used a lot of wood, and as the population of Philadelphia grew and the city spread out across the countryside, trees were becoming scarce. Woodcutters now had to go up to thirty miles into the countryside to find trees to chop down. Ben was convinced that there must be a more efficient way to heat homes. He came up with a design for a semienclosed cast-iron stove that he anticipated would use less wood while providing a more even heat.

The design consisted of nine iron plates that fit together to form a box that would fit into an existing fireplace. The stove had a pipe at the back that was designed to send all of the smoke up the chimney and the heat throughout the room. The heat was spread by a flue that doubled back to form a radiator on the top of the stove that gently heated the air around it.

When Ben finished the design, he hired Robert Grace, one of the original Junto Club members and an ironmonger, to make the prototype for him. Even Ben was surprised at how well the stove worked when he lit a fire in the prototype. After a few minor design changes, he ordered from Robert fifty of the stoves, which he had dubbed the "Pennsylvania Fireplace."

With the new stoves in hand, Ben used the *Pennsylvania Gazette* to advertise them. He wanted the wording of the advertisement to be just right, and after many drafts, he shrewdly decided that he could sell his new stoves best by appealing to colonial women's vanity. The final draft of his advertisement read:

Women, particularly from this cause [cold air] (as they sit much in the house) get colds in the head, rheums, and defluxions, which fall into their jaws and gums, and have destroyed many a fine set of teeth in these northern colonies. Great and bright fires also do very much to contribute to damage the eyes, dry and shrivel the skin, and bring on early the appearance of old age.

And the solution to all of these problems? The new Pennsylvania Fireplace.

By the winter of 1742 people were affectionately referring to the fireplace as the Franklin stove. After the first fifty stoves had been sold, Ben turned the production and sale of subsequent stoves over to Robert Grace. As word spread that the stove used only one cord of wood instead of four cords to warm a living room for an entire winter, more orders flooded in. Even the governor of Pennsylvania had several Franklin stoves installed in his mansion. He offered Ben a patent so that no one else could make a stove of that design without first paying Ben a royalty. Ben refused the governor's offer. He was much more interested in saving the trees and making people's lives easier. He also believed that every scientific inventor owed much of what he did to those who had made earlier discoveries and inventions. So, instead of issuing Ben a patent, the governor invited the entire colony of Pennsylvania to recognize Ben's achievement. In an official statement, he said, "Everybody can calculate what a saving this must be in one of the most necessary articles of house-keeping, and I believe all who have experienced the comfort and benefit of them [Ben's new stove] will join with me, that the author of this happy invention merits a statue from his countrymen."

In May 1743, with the invention of the Franklin stove behind him, Ben turned his attention in another direction by publishing a pamphlet titled *A Proposal for Promoting Useful Knowledge Among the British Plantations in America.* In this publication Ben wrote, "The first drudgery of settling new colonies, which confines the attention of people to mere necessities, is now pretty well over. And there are many in every province in circumstances that set them at ease, and afford leisure to cultivate the finer arts and improve the stock of knowledge." He then proposed that a "society be formed of Virtuosi or ingenious men residing in the several colonies, to be called The American Philosophical Society."

Ben went on to propose that this society be based in Philadelphia, since the roads from and through the other colonies all converged on the city. Philadelphia also had a thriving library, which would be necessary for such a society. In Philadelphia would reside a number of men with expertise in various disciplines, such as medicine, botany, mathematics, geography, chemistry, and natural science. These men would meet together once a month to discuss their latest findings and review information and results of scientific experiments sent in by members of the society located in other colonies. The best of this information would then be disseminated to the other members of the society.

After the publication of his proposal, Ben waited to see the scientists' reactions. He was encouraged when he received a long letter from Cadwallader Colden in New York. Colden was a trained doctor who now served as the surveyor general of New York. He was also one of the most eminent scientists in the American colonies. He encouraged Ben, offering to do anything he could to help the society get started. Other scientists and learned men in the American colonies gave their support to the idea, and in early 1744 the society was set up, with Ben serving as its secretary.

During the time that Ben was planning The American Philosophical Society, Debby informed him that he also needed to be planning for something else—another baby, who was due in September. Ben was surprised by the news. By now William was twelve years old, and it had been seven years since Francis had died. Ben had all but given up hope of ever being a father again. And now that it seemed he was going to be, Ben prayed for the safe delivery of a healthy child. His prayers were answered with the arrival of Sarah Franklin, who was born right on time in September. Sarah was nicknamed Sally from the start, and Ben chuckled to himself as he watched her grow—his little daughter looked so much like him.

Soon after Sally's birth, Ben hired a new foreman for the print shop. David Hall was from Scotland, and he was a hard worker and a skilled craftsman. With David overseeing the print shop, Ben felt free to spend more of his time on scientific pursuits. Now that he was corresponding with many other scientists throughout the colonies, his mind was spinning with theories and experiments to test them.

During 1744 Doctor Archibald Spencer showed up in Philadelphia. Ben had met him the year before on a trip to Boston to see his parents. Dr. Spencer, a Scotsman, was an "electrician," a showman who traveled around performing "magic" shows using electricity. So when he set up to do one of his shows in Philadelphia, Ben, along with many others in town, arrived to watch. In the course of his show, Dr. Spencer rubbed a glass rod to build up a static electric charge and then used the rod to attract pieces of gold and brass leaf. People gasped as the small pieces of metallic leaf were "magically" drawn across the tabletop toward the rod. After carrying out a number of such tricks, Dr. Spencer announced that he had saved the best for last and pulled back a curtain. There, suspended by silk cords from the ceiling, was a young boy. With great fanfare the doctor rubbed his glass rod vigorously for several minutes, then held it near the boy's feet. Following this, he put his fingers close to the boy's face and hand. Sparks lit the air. The crowd went wild as the "sparks of fire" came out of the boy's cheeks and hand.

Ben was spellbound by Archibald Spencer's demonstration of electricity. He also had recently read of Abbé Nollet in France, who had entertained King Louis XV by lining up 180 soldiers. Nollet had the soldiers all hold on to a piece of wire and then sent an electrical charge down the wire, causing all 180 soldiers to involuntarily jump simultaneously into the air. Reading of this and seeing Dr. Spencer's demonstration got Ben thinking about electricity. What was it? Where did it come from? And more important, was it good for anything? Did electricity have more practical uses than inducing sparks from a boy's cheeks or getting a line of French soldiers to jump into the air?

Ben decided that he would take some time to study electricity and its properties. Before Dr. Spencer left Philadelphia, Ben bought his entire bag of tricks, including the glass rods and tubes and wires. He turned his study at home into a laboratory to study electricity. He set up Dr. Spencer's equipment, along with a pewter saltshaker, an iron pump handle, and five brass thimbles from Debby's sewing box. Soon afterward Ben added a Leyden jar to his collection. This was a large glass jar coated inside and out with metal foil and with a large rubber stopper through which passed a copper rod, its tip resting just on the foil at the bottom of the jar. The Leyden jar was in fact an early capacitor, able to hold a single electric charge.

Once he had set himself up, Ben wrote to Peter Collinson, a botanist and the Library Company's agent in London. He asked Peter to send a larger glass rod to rub to generate current and any books or pamphlets having to do with electricity. Ben was delighted when several weeks later a glass rod three feet long and as thick as a man's wrist came in the mail. He immediately set to work experimenting with electricity.

One of the first things Ben discovered was that electric current flowed better through some materials than through others. Since no special words existed to describe the properties of electricity, Ben used words that he thought made sense. He called materials that electricity flowed through easily "conductors." The best conductors he discovered were metals and water. Material that resisted the flow of an electric current, such as wood, glass, and silk, he called "insulators." He also discovered that electric current could flow steadily in one direction, or it could alternate, changing direction and flowing back and forth. Ben chose the terms *positive* and *negative* to describe the amount of electricity in or on an object. He wrote in this regard, "We say *B* (and other bodies alike circumstanced) are electrised *positively; A negatively.* Or rather *B* is electrised *plus* and *A minus.*" Ben also improved on the Leyden jar, in the process producing an early electrical battery, using the reaction between two different metals to produce the charge. In this way he was able to get two or more spark-producing charges from the battery rather than just the single charge from the Leyden jar.

As he worked away, Ben kept precise notes of the experiments he conducted. He also wrote long letters to Peter, explaining in detail what he was doing and describing his findings and his hypotheses about electricity. Peter was a member of the Royal Society, and he in turn showed Ben's letters to some of the most eminent scientists in England. Much to Ben's delight, these scientists were very impressed with his research on electricity. They encouraged him for being such an imaginative thinker and for coming up with innovative experiments to test his hypotheses.

As Ben experimented more, the people of Philadelphia were fascinated by what he was up to. They would gather outside his house and peer into the windows to see what he was doing. Most of the time Ben was good-natured about the intrusion and usually put on a show for his audience, rubbing one of his glass rods to produce a charge to create sparks or using the charged rod to lead a small fish made of gold foil around his desk. At other times Ben did not want to be disturbed. On those occasions he had rigged up a surprise for the spectators who gathered around his house. As they hung from his wrought-iron fence, trying to get a good look in the windows at what he was doing, Ben would send an electrical charge down a wire outside his window, across the lawn, and to the iron fence. The people hanging on to the fence would get a mild electric shock, causing them to leap off it. This dampened their enthusiasm for a while, but they were back the next day, ready to see more electrical tricks.

Through his correspondence with Peter, Ben soon learned that his electrical discoveries were being compared to the discoveries of Sir Isaac Newton regarding gravity and the movement of the planets. Ben could scarcely believe the comparison. After all, he had barely two years of formal education, and he had only just begun his experiments.

As spring gave way to summer in Philadelphia and it became too hot to be cooped up in a laboratory experimenting, Ben proposed to hold a spectacle on the banks of the Schuylkill River. Among other things, he intended to send an electrical charge across the river, using the water as the conductor. The finale of the evening was to be the killing and cooking of a turkey using only electric current. Ben had already experimented with killing turkeys this way, and he had found that the electric current not only killed the birds but also relaxed their muscles and, as a result, made their meat very tender. However, Ben had also learned that it took quite a jolt of electric current to kill a bird as large as a turkey and that if the jolt was not big enough, it simply rendered the bird unconscious, and the bird would revive after a few minutes.

As the finale approached, Ben prepared for it. He had stored a large electrical charge in two Leyden jars, more than enough to kill a turkey, and was busy wrapping two wires together to tap the power of the two jars. As he worked away, people peppered him with questions about electricity, distracting him from what he was doing. And being distracted, Ben was still holding the ends of the two bare wires when the other ends touched the Leyden jars. A massive charge from the jars went straight through Ben, knocking him semiconscious to the ground. After a few minutes Ben clambered to his feet and dusted himself off. The people standing around were amazed that he was still alive. They had heard a large, crackling sound and had seen sparks burst from Ben's chest and the metal buckles of his shoes before he slumped to the ground. Ben recalled none of it, but the sparks explained the soreness he felt in his chest and feet. He was embarrassed to have been so careless, and he had to admit that his guests appeared to have enjoyed watching him getting electrocuted much more than witnessing the death of a turkey.

As he made his way home, with William at his side carrying much of the equipment, Ben promised himself that he would pay more attention in the future to what he was doing with electricity. It was more powerful than he had imagined, probably powerful enough to kill a man under the right circumstances.

Chapter 11

Time to Retire

When Debby informed Ben that sixteen-year-old William was missing, Ben was sure that he knew where to find his son. As fast as he could, Ben made his way to the docks that ran along the edge of the Delaware River. Debby, with baby Sally bundled in her arms, followed along behind. The riverfront was abuzz with ships bringing goods to Philadelphia and taking them from the city to ports all over the world. Also, many privateers were tied up along the docks, waiting to put to sea in the hope of capturing a haul of booty from some unsuspecting French ship, since France was England's current foe. Knowing how restless William had been lately, Ben was confident that his son would be trying to talk his way onto one of these ships, lured by tales of excitement and riches.

Ben asked around, and sure enough, he was directed to a small privateer docked at the end of a wharf. Ben climbed aboard the vessel, where he found William in a cabin below deck. William refused to budge, telling Ben that he had already signed on to the crew, but Ben would have none of it. He grabbed his son's knapsack of belongings and marched him back home.

As they headed up Market Street toward the house, Ben found it impossible to stay angry with William. How could he? After all, he had experienced the same restless urge to run away from Boston and his parents when he was seventeen years old. William had merely been following his example.

But it was not only William. It seemed to Ben that most young men in the American colonies were restless. And they had a right to be. The colonies were in an uproar over the latest clashes between the British and the French. From before the time Ben was born, the two nations had been arguing over who owned what part of North America and the islands of the Caribbean, and every few years the argument boiled over into armed conflict. The fact that the Indian tribes backed one side or the other made matters worse, as the combination of European land lust and the Indians' knowledge of the land made for some bloody conflicts.

A year before, in November 1745, a band of three hundred French soldiers and two hundred of their Indian allies had swept down from Canada and attacked the village of Saratoga in New York.

The village had no defenses, and thirty of its residents were killed and scalped, and another sixty were taken away as slaves. The intruders then razed Saratoga. The attack served as a chilling warning to the British, and the governor of Massachusetts petitioned King George II to allow the British colonies to seek revenge and invade Canada and push the French out. The king agreed, and as a result, each colony was expected to raise troops to march north to participate in the attack. At first the Pennsylvania Assembly had objected to raising troops, but it then relented and reluctantly called for volunteers.

Convinced that William would not be happy until he had made his own way in life, Ben suggested that he sign up to fight the French. He reasoned that a war on land was probably safer than going to sea on a privateer. William jumped at the opportunity, and soon he was Ensign William Franklin marching north to Albany, New York, where he would join the other fighting colonists.

Although, at forty, Ben felt no desire to go and fight, he was concerned about the threat of an attack in Pennsylvania, either from the French or from the Indian tribes that allied themselves with them. Because of his position as the clerk of court, Ben knew that the Indian threat was partly the fault of Thomas Penn. Sixty-five years before, at the founding of Pennsylvania, William Penn had taken great pains to respect the local Indians. He had dealt fairly with them and had become a great friend of theirs.

Thomas Penn and his brothers, however, were not interested in continuing their father's legacy of fairness and justice to all. As soon as he took control of the colony, Thomas began exploiting the Indians. One agreement that William Penn had made with the Delaware Indians was that he owned an amount of land called a "Walking Purchase." Since the land was not surveyed, everyone agreed that Penn could have the land that extended as far as a man could walk in a day and a half. It was widely assumed to be about thirty miles. When years later Thomas Penn read the contract his father had made with the Delawares, he set out to see just how much land he could wangle off the tribe. He advertised for the three fastest runners in the colony, cleared a path for them, and selected the longest day of the year for them to claim their "Walking Purchase." The result was predictable: the three men ran, not walked, and covered sixty-five miles from sun-up one day to noon the next. The Delaware Indians let Thomas Penn keep the land, but the bond between them and white men was broken as a result.

In 1747 Ben felt it was time for the Quakers and other residents of Pennsylvania to admit that the trust their founder had brokered with the Indians had been destroyed. Pennsylvania was as vulnerable as any of the other colonies and had to figure out a way to defend itself. But this position was made more difficult because the Quakers were pacifists and did not believe in bearing arms, even to defend themselves against attack.

As usual, Ben used the printing press to get his point across. He wrote and published a booklet titled *Plain Truth: Or, Serious Considerations on the Present State of the City of Philadelphia and the Province of Pennsylvania.* In the booklet he urged Pennsylvanians to band together and form militias to protect themselves from attack. The two thousand booklets Ben printed sold quickly, and he was forced to print more. And the booklet was having an effect. Soon a thousand men had volunteered to train for a militia. Ben was voted colonel of the Philadelphia regiment, but since he had no military background, he declined the position.

Now that he had inspired men to join the militia, Ben was faced with another challenge—where to get cannons to use to protect against attack from the river. Since all of the colonies felt vulnerable after the attack on Saratoga, none of them had any cannons to spare. Undaunted, Ben set up a lottery to raise three thousand pounds to buy cannons. When he had raised the money, he led a delegation north to New York to meet with Governor George Clinton. At first the governor laughed at their request to buy cannons, but Ben was a very persuasive man. Eventually Governor Clinton agreed to sell eighteen of New York's cannons to Ben.

Meanwhile Ben received a letter from William, who explained that his company was stuck in Albany, New York, apparently as the result of some bickering among the officers, who could not agree on how to proceed. William wrote about the moldy rations and the flimsy tents that offered little protection against the bitter winds. Nonetheless he sounded cheerful and reported that he had been promoted to captain and given a new assignment. His new assignment involved rounding up deserters and bringing them back to camp to face court-martial. Ben's heart sank as he read the letter. He had hoped that William would grow tired of the soldier's life and come home. Instead, despite the hardships, William seemed to be treating it like a grand adventure.

Within weeks of Ben's coming back from purchasing the cannons in New York, the British declared that the colonial war was over, at least for the present. And much to Ben's delight, William came home. But instead of settling down, William announced that he had joined an expedition going to the Ohio Valley to negotiate with the Indians.

Ben had no choice but to let William go. He had always hoped that William would take over the printing business, but now Ben realized that his only son had a taste for adventure, which the daily routine of the print shop would not satisfy. Ben knew it was time for him to make other plans for his own future.

At forty-two years of age, Ben decided to retire from the print shop. David Hall not only had turned out to be an excellent printer with a reputation for producing high-quality work but also had mastered the business side of running the print shop. Ben made David an equal partner in the business. They agreed that David would run the print shop and that David and Ben would split both the yearly costs and the profit from the business. At the end

of eighteen years, David would have the right to buy
out Ben's share of the printing business at its 1748
price. When the contract was signed, Ben Franklin's
days as a printer were over.

In September 1748 Ben wrote to his fellow scientist, Cadwallader Colden:

> I am in a fair way of having no other tasks
> than such as I shall like to give myself and of
> enjoying what I look upon as a great happi-
> ness, leisure to read, study, and make exper-
> iments, and converse at large with such
> ingenious and worthy men as are pleased to
> honor me with their friendship and acquain-
> tance, on such points as may produce some-
> thing for the common benefit of mankind,
> uninterrupted by the little cares and fatigues
> of business.

The experiment foremost on Ben Franklin's mind
had to do with the most mysterious of natural
occurrences—the nature of lightning.

Chapter 12

Kite Flying

Although Ben intended to spend his future in scientific pursuits, other events claimed much of his time. His first task was to move his family into a new house he had rented. The house was located on the corner of Race and Second Streets, nearer to the river and in a much quieter part of town than the house on Market Street. Ben had just finished moving into the place when he learned that he had been nominated to serve in the Pennsylvania Assembly, the governing body of the colony. This was a great honor, especially for someone who was born and raised in another colony. Ben wrote immediately to his family in Boston, telling them the news.

In response, Ben's mother wrote, "I am glad to hear you are so well respected in your toun for them to chuse you alderman alltho I dont know what it means nor what the better you will be of it beside the honer of it. I hope you will look up to God and thank him for all his good providences toward you."

As a result of serving in the assembly, Ben found himself being drawn more deeply into civic affairs. He kept imagining ways to improve people's lives and then focused on turning those dreams into reality. One of Ben's visions was for a first-rate school for boys in the city. Until then, promising boys had been sent off to England as teenagers to be educated. Ben saw this as a wasted opportunity, since some of the brightest boys never returned to the colony. Opportunities were also wasted because poor boys, even the smartest ones, had no free school to attend. In response Ben set up the Philadelphia Academy and Charitable School. The school was open to any boy who showed intellectual promise, no matter how little money his family had. A twenty-four-member board was chosen to oversee the running of the school, and Ben was elected its president.

With the school functioning well, Ben turned his attention to another pressing need in the community: a public hospital. There were no hospitals in the American colonies. If a rich person got sick, he hired someone to take care of him in his home. If a poor person got sick, he waited to either recover on his own or die.

Dr. Thomas Bond approached Ben for help with the idea of building a public hospital, and Ben threw himself into the project. He used the *Pennsylvania Gazette* to popularize the idea and to raise money for it. His efforts were more successful than even Ben had hoped they would be. In 1752 the first patient was admitted to the new twenty-bed hospital in Philadelphia. The hospital was overseen by one doctor and had a free drug dispensary. Soon representatives from the other colonies were visiting Philadelphia to see how the hospital was run.

As he had done when nominated to the Pennsylvania Assembly, Ben wrote home to tell his mother the good news about the new hospital. The return letter he received from Boston brought sad news. Ben's mother had died. Now both his parents were dead. Josiah Franklin, his father, had died seven years before. Ben was sorry that neither of his parents was able to celebrate his latest achievements.

When his time was not occupied with assembly and civic matters, Ben turned his attention to the thing he wanted to do most—study electricity and, in particular, the nature of lightning. The idea that lightning might be electrical had been put forward by Sir Isaac Newton nearly fifty years before, but no one had ever proved it. Ben set out to be the first. He wrote to the Royal Society in London, suggesting an experiment to decide the matter. "On the top of some high tower or steeple," he wrote, "place a kind of sentry box big enough to contain a man and an electrical stand. From the middle of the stand let an iron rod rise, and pass bending out of the door, and then upright 20 or 30 feet, pointed very sharp at the end. If the electrical stand be kept clean and dry a man standing on it when such clouds are passing low, might be electrified, and afford sparks, the rod drawing fire to him from the cloud."

The problem in Pennsylvania, and in fact the entire colonies of North America, was that no buildings existed that Ben considered high enough from which to carry out the experiment himself. Ben decided to wait for the new spire at Christ Church in Philadelphia to be erected, since he thought that this would be high enough. However, as construction of the spire dragged on, Ben became impatient. He wanted to find out once and for all whether or not lightning was an electric charge. He would lie awake at night trying to think of some experiment that would achieve the same result.

Finally it dawned on Ben. He did not need a high building from which to conduct his experiment; a kite could fly high into the sky! Ben enlisted the help of twenty-two-year-old William, who was home taking a break from his adventures in the Ohio Valley. The two of them constructed a kite from a large silk handkerchief. To the top of the kite they attached a foot-long metal spike. The kite was attached to a long hemp cord, a reasonable conductor of electricity when dry, and excellent when it was wet. To the end of the cord was attached another silk handkerchief, which the kite flyer would hold and thus be isolated from the electric charge should there be one. A metal key was attached near the bottom of the hemp cord by a ribbon. With the kite built, father and son waited for just the right storm to pass over Philadelphia.

Finally, late one afternoon in June 1752, a thunderstorm approached Philadelphia. Ben and William took their kite and headed for a field outside of town. By the time they got there, rain was pouring down. Ben took shelter in a small shepherd's hut in the field while William ran back and forth in the rain three times before the kite finally took flight. As the kite climbed into the sky, William let out the hemp cord. When all the cord had been played out, he went to the shepherd's hut and handed the cord to his father. It was all up to Ben now.

Standing in the doorway of the hut, Ben carefully guided the kite, avoiding the large forks of lightning that blazed across the sky. Finally a low storm cloud made its way over the field. Ben guided the kite into the cloud. When the blackness of the cloud had completely engulfed the kite, Ben reached up and touched the key. He felt nothing. Could his hypothesis be wrong? Could lightning not be an electrical charge, after all? As he pondered what to make of this result, Ben noticed that the loose threads on the hemp cord were standing on end. It could mean only one thing—the threads were electrically charged. As Ben carefully reached out to touch the key a second time, sparks arched between his knuckles and the key, and a jolt of electricity pulsed through him. Joy overtook Ben. He had done it! Lightning and electricity were one and the same after all.

Ben reeled in the kite, and he and William went home to change into dry clothes and celebrate their achievement.

It was not until a letter arrived five months later from Thomas-François d'Alibard in France that Ben realized the Frenchman had beaten him. On May 10, 1752, d'Alibard reported that he had completed the experiment as Ben had suggested it on top of a church spire on the outskirts of Paris. Just as Ben had predicted, an electrical spark had traveled down the rod. The news of the experiment, which proved that electricity occurred in nature as lightning, reverberated throughout Europe.

Whether in France or in Pennsylvania, Ben was glad that his point had been proven once and for all. Now came the part Ben liked best—thinking of practical uses that could result from his scientific experiments with electricity. Although he wondered whether passing an electric current through a person could cure paralysis, fainting fits, and deafness, he concentrated on how to prevent lightning strikes from killing people and setting buildings on fire. Ben's answer came during a storm, when he saw lightning strike the highest point of a house and travel down through the metal fixtures to the ground. Immediately Ben began experimenting with tall, pointed metal rods that could be fixed to the top of a building to draw lightning. He attached the lightning rod to a wire that ran down the side of the building to the ground, where the electricity dissipated.

To Ben's surprise, his idea of installing lightning rods on buildings was vehemently opposed by some prominent clergymen, who believed that God used lightning to judge men and that interfering with lightning would bring down God's wrath on all of them. Others suggested that if lightning were drawn into the earth, it would surely build up there, causing massive earthquakes. Despite these dire predictions, most people were eager to erect lightning rods on their houses. They followed Ben's advice about staying away from tall objects such as trees during thunderstorms. As a result, the death rate from being struck by lightning went down rapidly.

Ben printed a booklet containing his findings and included instructions on how to make a lightning rod in the 1753 *Poor Richard's Almanack*. That same year both Yale and Harvard Universities awarded Ben honorary degrees, followed in 1754 by the Royal Society's giving him the Copley Gold Medal for his work on electricity.

Ben was also appointed to the position of deputy postmaster general of all the American colonies, while William took over Ben's role as postmaster of Pennsylvania. Ben's new position sounded important, but in fact it paid only 150 pounds a year. Ben and the new postmaster of the colonies, William Hunter of Virginia, invested 900 pounds of their own money to redesign the postal service. Ben set out on a ten-week inspection tour of post offices throughout the colonies. He was astonished at the different ways mail was handled in the various places, and he made plans to improve them.

Within six months of Ben's taking up his new position, the postal service was much more efficient. Mail was now delivered three times a week between Philadelphia and New York, instead of once a week, and twice a week between the New England colonies and Philadelphia. For a penny, a person could have mail delivered to his or her home or business. Ben also set up an office in Philadelphia to handle all dead letters—letters that could not be delivered. For the first time ever, the colonial post offices turned a profit.

One of the benefits of being deputy postmaster general was that Ben was one of the few men on the continent who knew people in all thirteen colonies. Ben's acquaintances provided him with a constant supply of funny stories to tell. His own favorite story to tell was about the time in Rhode Island when he stopped at a tavern for the night. Alas, he found that twenty other travelers were already huddled around the fireplace. Ben was cold and wet, but no one made room for him to warm himself. That was when he spotted the tavern keeper's son. "Boy," he yelled, "fetch my horse a quart of oysters."

"A quart of oysters?" the boy questioned.

"That's what I said," Ben replied. "Your best quart of oysters."

The boy hurried to the bar and produced a bucket of oysters. As he headed out the door, everyone in the room followed, eager to see the amazing oyster-eating horse. Ben chuckled to himself as they left and he spread out his jacket to dry in front of the fire. A minute later everyone returned. "Sir," the boy said, "your horse won't eat the oysters."

"Oh?" Ben said. "In that case, bring me the oysters and give my horse some hay."

By that time the other travelers realized that they had been duped out of their places by the fire, but they could not get angry with Ben. Instead they all crowded back in, laughing at the way he had fooled them all.

As Ben went about his new job, clouds were gathering over the colonies that no one was laughing about. England and France were fighting again. The situation had not yet officially been called a war, but the signs were all there. The English and the Iroquois Indians were fighting the French and their Indian allies for domination of the Ohio Valley.

Just as before, a strategy was needed to defend the colonies against the French and Indians. In 1754 each colony sent representatives to Albany, New York, to come up with a plan. Ben was chosen as one of the representatives from Pennsylvania, and he used the opportunity to introduce something he had been pondering for quite some time. He called it the Albany Plan of Union, which advocated the creation of a governor general of all of the colonies and a grand council chosen from each colony's assembly. This new council would have the right to raise taxes to build forts and supply the militias that would protect all of the colonies. Furthermore, he suggested that since the colonists lived where the fighting was likely to take place, they should be the ones who made the decisions about how best to defend themselves and seek the approval of the British government.

It all made perfect sense to Ben Franklin, especially since he was already dealing with all of the colonies as deputy postmaster general. Ben even drew and printed the first cartoon to appear in a newspaper to illustrate his point. The cartoon was of a snake chopped into pieces, with each piece bearing the initials of one of the colonies. Underneath he had written the words, "Join or Die." In Ben's opinion the message was clear: either the colonies join together to form a council to fight the French and Indians, or they would all die.

The delegates from the other colonies did not see it Ben's way. They were shocked by how much power Ben suggested each colony give up to this governing body, and they accused him of being an "arrant blockhead." None of the other representatives seemed to understand Ben's goal of getting the colonies to work together, or so it appeared to Ben, who lamented, "Everyone cries, a union is absolutely necessary; but when they come to the manner and form their weak noodles [brains] are distracted."

Still, Ben did not give up. Deep in his heart he knew that the time would come when the colonies would have to learn to cooperate and rely on each other rather than wait for months for instructions to arrive across the Atlantic Ocean from England. He just did not know what that change would cost him and everyone else in the colonies.

Chapter 13

An Official Representative

While Ben and the other representatives from the colonies had been meeting together in Albany, across the Allegheny Mountains at a hastily built stockade named Fort Necessity, fighting was taking place. A force of Virginia militiamen under the command of Colonel George Washington had been sent to stop the French from building a fort at the confluence of the Monongahela and Allegheny Rivers. However, this military action had been poorly organized. Militia troops promised from New York failed to show up on time, and eventually a combined force of Indians and French soldiers had forced Washington to surrender to save all of the men under his command from being slaughtered.

Ben learned of this debacle when he arrived back in Philadelphia from Albany. Soon afterward the British government announced that it was sending two regiments of soldiers to march across the Allegheny Mountains and destroy Fort Duquesne, which George Washington had been unable to stop the French from building.

The British troops under the command of Major General Edward Braddock arrived at Alexandria, Virginia, from England in March 1755. By May 2 they were encamped at Frederick, Maryland, their staging ground before heading west over the Alleghenies. When General Braddock arrived in Frederick, he was furious to find only twenty-five wagonloads of supplies waiting for his men. He fumed that the leaders of the colonies had promised to supply him many times that amount, and he demanded something be done about it. As a result, Ben Franklin, the deputy postmaster general, was dispatched to try to smooth things out with General Braddock.

Ben noticed that the general seemed to enjoy his company, though he himself found General Braddock to be arrogant, cantankerous, and hard to please. Even so, he did his best to get along with the general, agreeing to secure 150 wagons with four horses to pull each wagon, as well as 260 riding and pack horses. The general advanced Ben eight hundred pounds, to which Ben added two hundred pounds of his own money, to pay as bonds to the farmers for the use of their wagons and horses.

Two weeks later Ben, with the help of William, had collected the wagons and horses and escorted them to Frederick. General Braddock was delighted, describing Ben as "almost the only Instance of Ability and Honesty I have known in these Provinces." The comment embarrassed Ben, since he thought most of his fellow colonists were able and honest.

When he arrived at the British encampment this second time, Ben met Colonel George Washington, who was acting as an adviser to General Braddock. Washington was a tall, handsome man who spoke forthrightly and had a commanding presence about him. The contrast between him and General Braddock could not have been more pronounced, and Ben was greatly impressed by him.

Before he left, Ben encouraged General Braddock to plan his attack on Fort Duquesne very carefully. He pointed out that the French and the Indians on the American frontier had adapted their fighting to take advantage of trees, ravines, and rocky outcrops. They did not follow "gentlemanly rules of engagement" but used whatever methods they could to kill their enemies. In Europe, where the general had gained his experience, both sides lined their troops up in orderly formation on the field of battle and attacked on signal.

General Braddock smiled condescendingly and replied, "These savages may indeed be a formidable enemy to your raw American militia, but upon the king's regulars and disciplined troops, sir, it is impossible they should make an impression."

Although Ben found General Braddock's arrogant attitude repugnant, he hoped for the sake of the troops that the general knew what he was doing.

General Braddock would have been wise to have taken Ben's advice. Ben and William were back in Philadelphia when they heard the devastating news. Not only had the French and Indians defeated General Braddock and his men, but two-thirds of the British officers, including the general, and half of his men had been killed in the fighting. Ben was not surprised to learn that George Washington had emerged as the hero of the whole ordeal, leading the survivors to safety.

The news sent a chill through the city, and especially through Ben, who had put up bonds guaranteeing the safe return of the wagons and horses the British forces had used. If the British government refused to honor those bonds and pay up what was owed for the destruction of the wagons and the horses, Ben would be forced to pay the twenty thousand pounds out of his own money, an amount that would financially ruin him.

As Ben set about petitioning the new governor to pay the money owed, more shocking news arrived from the western frontier. Some of the Iroquois Indians, who traditionally sided with the English, had switched sides and were now fighting with the French. They had crossed the Alleghenies and had sacked several farmhouses on the eastern side of the mountains. In addition, a band of Shawnee Indians had murdered all the inhabitants of the Moravian village of Gnadenhutten, just seventy miles from Philadelphia. The French and Indian War, as the hostilities were now being termed, was on their doorstep. Suddenly Ben's warning about joining together or dying took on a new urgency.

The Pennsylvania Assembly argued that much more had to be done and adopted the bill Ben proposed to create a government-backed militia to defend the colony. Forts and stockades had to be hastily constructed. Ben took command of fifty cavalrymen and headed north to fortify the Moravian settlement of Bethlehem. It was there on January 17, 1756, that he passed his fiftieth birthday directing the building of stockades, with twenty-six-year-old William at his side. The men worked feverishly. It was a matter of life or death for their communities. Other unprecedented measures were also taken. While many Quaker pacifists protested and sought a peaceful solution in the tradition of William Penn, the Pennsylvania Assembly offered a bounty to any settler who killed a male Indian and turned in his scalp.

When the fortifications were complete, Ben and William returned to Philadelphia, where Ben took up the prickly issue of how the war effort was to be financed. Pennsylvania belonged to the Penn family. The family owned huge tracts of land on which they never paid taxes because, they argued, they would only be paying themselves. But in the face of this present crisis, the people of Pennsylvania began to take a long, hard look at their government. Why should they pay to defend the Penn family's estates, when the Penns, who were enormously wealthy, did not contribute a penny of their own money? It was a good question, and one that Ben took up in the assembly.

Of course, it was not really the assembly that Ben had to convince but the Penn family itself. Not surprisingly, the Penn family members were unwilling to contribute to the defense of their lands. By May 1757 things had reached an impasse, and the assembly decided to send a representative to England to argue its case before the king and Parliament that the Penns should pay taxes like everyone else in the colony. The man they chose for the job was Ben Franklin.

Ben, for his part, was delighted to be off to England again, accompanied by his son, William. And he was even more delighted when he learned just hours before boarding the packet ship that would carry them to London that the government had finally decided to honor its financial obligation for property destroyed in General Braddock's disastrous campaign. Ben would not be financially ruined after all.

As the ship headed out into the Atlantic Ocean, Ben reflected on how far he had come since his previous voyage to England thirty-three years ago. Back then he had thought he was off to do the governor's bidding, but all his dreams had turned to ashes. Now he was a famous scientist, and as an official representative of the governing assembly of Pennsylvania, he was on his way to negotiate with the most powerful men in the world on behalf of the colony.

The voyage across the Atlantic was perilous. French warships patrolled the sea lanes, and for the first time, Ben was grateful for the heavy fog that shrouded the ship for most of the journey. And then, as they neared the English shoreline, the crew lost sight of the Falmouth lighthouse. The ship narrowly missed a rocky outcrop before the fog cleared and the light shined through. Ben made a mental note to promote the building of lighthouses along the North American eastern seaboard.

Despite these perils, the ship finally docked safely at Falmouth in late July 1757. From Falmouth Ben hurried off on the nine-day coach journey to London. One of the first people he met there was his old pen pal Peter Collinson. Since the days of his experiments with electricity, Ben had corresponded with Peter regularly.

Peter helped Ben find lodging at the home of a widow, Margaret Stevenson, and her daughter Polly at 36 Craven Street, Charing Cross. The situation suited Ben well. The house was close to Whitehall, where government was conducted, and Fleet Street, which was the printing district. William lived in the house with Ben, though he decided to study law instead of acting as his father's full-time secretary, as had been originally planned.

Before Ben did anything else in London, he took note of the latest fashions. The men were wearing silver-buckled shoes and long wigs, and Ben and William had soon outfitted themselves in such attire so as not to look like they had just arrived from the colonies.

At first Ben had imagined that he would be in London for only a few months, but he soon learned that the Penn family had no intention of paying taxes on their estates in their colony, and no one in Parliament or the Royal Court seemed to care much.

In fact, when Ben went to see Lord Granville, the head of the Privy Council, which in turn answered to King George II, he was told that the Pennsylvania Assembly had fewer legal powers than it believed it had. The assembly had always held that it had the power to veto a decision of the king regarding the colony if it thought that the decision was not in the best interests of Pennsylvania. But according to Lord Granville, this was not so. The king's decisions were final and binding and could and would be enforced in the colony, with military backing if need be. This news shocked Ben, and he wondered how he was going to make any headway at all in getting the government in London to change its mind with regard to the Penns' paying an equitable amount of the colony's tax burden.

The months slipped by, and Ben found himself celebrating Christmas in England. He sent home lavish gifts of china and linen to Debby and Sally, whom he looked forward to seeing soon. A month later, when he realized it could take another year or more to make any progress, he wrote to Debby, asking her to come to England to be with him. Her reply was as Ben had expected it would be: Debby was deathly afraid of water and refused to set foot on any type of boat, not even to cross the Delaware or Schuylkill rivers, let alone the Atlantic Ocean.

Ben continued his maneuvering with the British government, though it was hard going. The king was reluctant to interfere with the Penns, who, after all, were the rightful owners of Pennsylvania.

In the spring Ben and William set off for the village of Ecton, in Northamptonshire. This was Ben's father's home village, and Ben was eager to see the old Franklin homestead his father and Uncle Benjamin had spoken of. When they arrived, Ben and William were greeted by a slew of distant relatives who were happy to show them the house, which had recently been turned into a school. Ben studied the family records on gravestones and at the local Anglican church. Much to his surprise, he discovered that he was the youngest son of the youngest son back through five generations. He also learned that most of his ancestors had been farmers, blacksmiths, and dyers, all worthy professions in Ben's eyes.

From Ecton, Ben and William ventured north to Scotland, where Ben was given an honorary degree of doctor of laws from the University of Saint Andrews. Ben rather liked the ring of the title "Dr. Franklin" that the degree conferred upon him and decided to use it from then on. From Scotland it was back to London and another session of arguing with the Privy Council.

Finally, in 1760, Ben struck a deal that he felt the Pennsylvania Assembly could live with. The king and the Privy Council agreed to let the assembly levy taxes on Penn family estates except for those estates that had not yet been properly surveyed.

Although it was tempting to go straight back to America after the deal was struck, Ben decided to stay in London and help William settle his future.

Meanwhile King George II died, and his grand-son, the next in line to the throne, became King George III. Ben was delighted to be invited to his coronation in October 1761. George III was only twenty-two years old, but Ben had high hopes that he would deal fairly with the colonies. He wrote home that the new king appeared to be the "very best in the world and the most amiable."

By 1762 everything seemed to be going well. William, with help from Ben's English friends, had been appointed the royal governor of New Jersey. His new title attracted a wife as well, Elizabeth Downes, the daughter of a wealthy sugar planter from Barbados.

Finally it was time for the Franklins to make their way back to North America. On August 23, 1762, Ben Franklin stood on the deck of the ship as it set sail for New York. He could hardly believe that he had been gone from Pennsylvania for over five years, and he wondered how much things there had changed in that time.

Chapter 14

Everyone Was Raising a Toast to Him

The voyage back across the Atlantic Ocean to North America was a slow one. The French and English were still at war with each other, and Ben's ship had to take its place in a slow-moving convoy of vessels. Still, Ben enjoyed his ten weeks aboard, though he was happy to reach New York. He was even happier when he finally got back to Philadelphia, where he found his house filled with people ready to renew their friendships with him.

On his arrival home, Ben noticed that Debby seemed older, and then laughed to himself when he realized that he had gone gray in the five years he'd been away! Their daughter, Sally, who was eighteen years old now, was an intelligent, spirited young woman. She loved to play the harpsichord, and Ben happily accompanied her on the violin.

Ben also noticed many changes in the city of Philadelphia. New buildings had gone up, and people told him that the streets had become more crowded with new immigrants. But being fresh from bustling London, to Ben the streets looked half empty.

As soon as he could, Ben made his way to the Assembly House to give a full accounting of his time in England and of the deal he had struck with King George and the Privy Council. He also reported that he thought the war between France and England would soon come to an end, as both countries were weary of fighting each other.

As it turned out, Ben was right. In November 1762 Great Britain and France began negotiating a peaceful settlement to their confrontation. The following February the settlement was finalized. Under the terms of the agreement, the British gained control of the French colony of New France to the north of the American colonies, giving the English control of Canada. In addition, the British gained control of the eastern half of the French territory of Louisiana and Florida. The French for their part gained control of two Caribbean islands, Guadeloupe and Martinique.

Now that Canada was a British colony, Ben's job as deputy postmaster general was to coordinate the mail from the other colonies to Montreal, Quebec, and beyond. Ben decided that the best way to achieve this was to take a five-month tour of all the post offices under his care. He set off in late spring 1763. He wanted to take Debby and Sally with him, but Debby refused to budge from Philadelphia. She was afraid of the streams and rivers they would have to cross on their journey, so Ben and Sally set out alone. They took a coach to New York, where Ben set up a central route so that mail could get from there to Philadelphia in one day and back the next. This extraordinarily speedy service required for the first time ever the use of nightriders, who rode their horses through the night to make sure the mail arrived on time.

From New York it was on to Boston, where Ben stayed with his sister Jane. Jane was the only one of his siblings still alive, and just thinking about that made Ben feel old. He felt even older when he was pitched from the horse he was riding and injured his right shoulder. It took a month for him to recover enough to mount his horse again and many more months before his shoulder completely healed.

When father and daughter returned to Philadelphia, Ben had the satisfaction of knowing that the postal service was running smoothly. However, other matters in the colonies were not going so well. With the war over, many of the colonists expected a long period of peace, but this was not the case. In the past, the Indian tribes had been protected in many ways through their alliances with the French or the British. But those days were over, and the Indians found themselves without allies. The British government tried to keep the settlers and the Indians apart as best they could because they did not want to foot the bill for protecting the settlers.

To aid them in this, they issued a proclamation declaring that settlers could not settle west of the Appalachian Mountains. But the settlers, eager to claim new land, simply refused to obey the proclamation. As a result, bloody conflicts arose as the settlers moved west and the Indians, under Chief Pontiac, tried to hold on to their traditional hunting grounds.

Ben understood the problem and explained it to the members of the Pennsylvania Assembly:

> The Indians are disgusted that so little notice has lately been taken of them, and [they] are particularly offended that rum is prohibited, and [gun] powder dealt among them so sparingly. They have received no presents. And the plan of preventing war among them, and bringing them to live by agriculture, they resent as an attempt to make women of them, as they phrase it, it being the business of women only to cultivate the ground. Their men are warriors.

Despite his understanding of the Indians' situation, Ben did not side with them. Instead, he urged the assembly to deal harshly with the Indians so that they would never forget the price of war with the settlers. However, even Ben was appalled at what happened next. In December 1763 a band of frontiersmen from the town of Paxton on the Susquehanna River attacked a band of Indians who were Moravian converts at nearby Conestoga. The men killed six of the innocent Indians and razed their houses. A few days later, the Paxton Boys, as they were being called, took matters into their own hands again, this time killing fourteen Indian men, women, and children. Next the Paxton Boys marched to the outskirts of Philadelphia, where some Quakers were sheltering 140 Indian converts.

The governor appealed to Ben to help him, and Ben advised him to stand firm against the Paxton Boys. Men and arms were gathered together, and Ben went off to Germantown to meet with the leaders of the mob. He managed to talk them out of advancing on Philadelphia, thus preventing a bloody confrontation.

When the Paxton Boys finally retreated, Ben took time to reflect on the situation. He was shocked that so-called civilized men could be transformed into a blood-lusting mob. He decided that the best way to try to stop such a thing from occurring again was with his pen. So in January 1764 he printed a pamphlet titled *A Narrative of the Late Massacres in Lancaster County, of a Number of Indians, Friends of This Province.* He wrote about how Shehaes, a very old Indian man and a friend of William Penn's, had been hatcheted to death, along with his daughter and her family. He ended the pamphlet with an impassioned plea:

> They fell on their knees, protested their innocence, declared their love to the English, and that, in their whole lives, they had never done them injury; and in this posture they

all received the hatchet! Women and little children—were every one inhumanly murdered!—in cold blood!... The guilt will lie on the whole land till justice is done on these murderers. THE BLOOD OF THE INNOCENT WILL CRY TO HEAVEN FOR VENGEANCE.

By the time the pamphlet was distributed, Ben had made himself a few new friends and a lot of new enemies. People were outraged that he would take the side of the Indians, and he and his family were attacked and mocked.

As a result of all this turmoil, Ben lost his seat in the Pennsylvania Assembly. However, he was soon appointed to a new position. The new assembly asked him to return to England to press once again for the king to take the colony away from the Penn family and move it from being a proprietorship to a royal colony.

Ben had mixed feelings about returning to London. He knew that there was no chance that Debby would join him, and although Sally was eager to go with him and be introduced to British society, Ben urged her to stay behind with her mother.

In early November 1764, after being home for two years, Ben set sail for England for a third time. Three hundred residents of Philadelphia gave him a rousing send-off, complete with a cannon salute. Ben waved at the crowd as he left and promised himself that he would do his best to free them from the reign of the Penn family.

When he arrived in London a month later, Ben discovered that he had more important things to be concerned about. On the surface things were much the same as they had been before. Ben settled back into his lodgings at Margaret Stevenson's house and visited his old friends on Fleet Street. But under the surface, a fire was smoldering. It had to do with the fact that the war between Britain and France was now over. The British had added up the amount the whole conflict had cost them, and Parliament and the Privy Council realized that they were seriously in debt. They began to look around for someone to help pay for the war, and their eyes settled on the American colonies. The leaders of government argued that since the war had been about protecting the colonies, the colonies should not only pay for the war but also pay for the high costs of maintaining peace with the Indians.

Just as Ben arrived in London, Parliament passed an act taxing sugar, coffee, and wine in the colonies. Then it broadened this out to a tax on every piece of paper used in the colonies, including books, land titles, almanacs, playing cards, wills, and licenses. To prove that the proper taxes had been paid on these items, a paper stamp was to be stuck onto each item before it was sold. The act that established these taxes was known as the Stamp Act.

When Ben realized that the British government was not going to be happy until it had extracted some money from the colonies, he spent his time lobbying Parliament to set the tax low and not get greedy. What he did not know was just how angry the people of Pennsylvania and the other American colonies were about the prospect of any tax being placed on them, especially without their being represented in the British parliament. So while Ben was trying to reason with the political leaders in England, the colonists were busy showing their anger at the mother country.

Ben was astounded when he learned that in Boston a mob had wrecked the stamp officer's house and burned his effigy in the streets. New England merchants had called for a boycott on all imported products. In Philadelphia a mob had even gathered outside his house, trying to force Debby out so that they could loot it. Debby had fended them off bravely with a shotgun until neighbors rallied to her aid. Ben could hardly imagine such a scene. And he found it hard to believe that a group calling itself the Sons of Liberty was organizing resistance to the British in towns throughout New England.

Ben continued to follow events at home through both imported newspapers and letters from friends and family. He learned that in October 1765 the Stamp Act Congress had met in New York to petition Britain to repeal the act. The congress had even gone so far as to write a Declaration of Rights and Grievances, a copy of which it had sent to everyone in the British government. When he read the declaration, Ben realized just how serious the matter of the Stamp Act had become in the colonies. It was time for him to act. He did everything he could think of in London to get the act repealed, from lobbying British merchants who had been hurt by the downturn in exports to the colonies to publishing sarcastic pamphlets making fun of the British attitudes toward the colonies.

Finally, in January 1766, the actions of Ben and several others forced the issue of the unpopularity of the Stamp Act to be investigated and debated in the House of Commons. About thirty witnesses, many of them merchants, were called to testify before the House of Commons, and Ben sat listening as they answered questions put to them by members of the Commons. Finally it was Ben's time to testify. He rose to his feet and stepped forward. The clerk of the House of Commons asked him to state his name and residence for the record.

"Franklin, of Philadelphia," Ben said respectfully.

The members of the House of Commons then began to pepper Ben with questions relating to the American colonies and their reaction to the Stamp Act. One member inquired as to what taxes American colonists already paid.

"Many, and very heavy taxes," Ben answered. "There are taxes on all estates real and personal; a poll tax; a tax on all offices, professions, trades, and businesses, according to their profits; an excise on all wine, rum, and other spirits; and a duty of ten pounds per head on all Negroes imported, with some other duties."

Another member asked about how easy it would be to distribute the tax stamps in the colonies. As deputy postmaster general, Ben had firsthand knowledge of the difficulties involved here, and he began to point them out.

"The posts go only along the sea coasts; they do not, except in a few instances, go back into the country; and if they did, sending for stamps by post would occasion an expense of postage amounting, in many cases, to much more than that of the stamps themselves."

Following every ounce of advice he had written in *Poor Richard's Almanack* about self-control, Ben patiently answered question after question. With each answer, Ben pushed forward his argument that the Stamp Act should be repealed.

"What was the temper of the Americans toward Great Britain before 1763?" another member of the Commons asked.

"The best in the world. They submitted willingly to the government of the Crown, and paid, in all their courts, obedience to acts of Parliament. Numerous as the people are in the several old provinces, they cost you nothing in forts, citadels, garrisons, or armies, to keep them in subjection. They were governed by this country at the expense only of a little pen, ink, and paper. They were led by a thread," Ben replied.

"And what is the temper of the Americans now?" the member asked in follow-up.

"Very much altered," Ben said.

"And in what light did the Americans regard Parliament?"

"As the great bulwark and security of their liberties and privileges," Ben answered.

"And do the Americans retain their respect for Parliament?"

"No, it is greatly lessened," came Ben's reply.

"Have the Americans formerly objected to Parliament's authority on the subjects of taxes and duties?"

"I never heard any objections to the right of laying duties to regulate commerce," Ben said. Then he added forthrightly, "But a right to lay internal taxes was never supposed to be in Parliament, as we are not represented here."

Another member of the House of Commons argued that whatever the names used, they were irrelevant, because, after all, a tax is a tax. He then asked Ben to explain why he thought the two were different.

"The difference is very great," Ben began. "An external tax is a duty laid on commodities imported; that duty is added to the first cost, and other charges on the commodity, and when it is offered to sale, makes a part of the price. If the people do not like it at that price, they refuse it; they are not obliged to pay it. But an internal tax is forced from the people without their consent, if not laid by their own representatives. The Stamp Act says we shall have no commerce, make no exchange of property with each other, neither purchase nor grant, nor recover debts; we shall neither marry nor make our wills unless we pay such and such sums, and thus it is intended to extort our money from us, or ruin us by the consequences of refusing to pay it."

"Could anything less than military force compel the Americans to accept the stamps?" another member asked.

"I do not see how a military force can be applied to that purpose," Ben responded.

"Why not?" snapped another member of the Commons.

"Suppose a military force is sent to America," Ben began. "They will find nobody in arms. What are they then to do? They cannot force a man to take stamps who chooses to do without them. They will not find a rebellion; they may indeed make one."

Finally, after four hours, the questioning was over, and Ben left the House of Commons. Despite some harassing questions from a few members of the House of Commons who seemed more intent on rattling him than getting to the bottom of the issue, Ben had felt at his best. His answers had been persuasive, and he was sure that he had influenced the minds of many parliamentarians to repeal the dreaded Stamp Act. And he was right. By a vote of 275 to 167, the Stamp Act was repealed. Ben hurriedly wrote to the members of the Pennsylvania Assembly, informing them of the outcome of the debate in the House of Commons. The return letter he received from the assembly described how he was now a hero in Philadelphia and everyone was raising a toast to him.

Other letters of congratulations followed. Ben also received letters from the leaders of Georgia, New Jersey, and Massachusetts, asking him to represent their colonies in London as well. With astonishing speed, Ben Franklin became the single most important voice for the colonies in England.

Ben turned sixty during the fight for the repeal of the Stamp Act. It was now eighteen years since he had entered into the business agreement with David Hall, and as agreed upon, David took full ownership of the print shop and the *Pennsylvania Gazette.*

Ben would no longer receive any income from the printing business he had founded. It became more important than ever for him to represent the American colonies well at Whitehall, since the money they now paid him to represent their interests was his and Debby's main source of income.

As months passed, Ben became increasingly frustrated with his new role. It seemed at times that the British parliament was so corrupt that he could not appeal to any member's conscience. To make matters worse, King George III, whom he had considered to be a very competent young man at his coronation, was now making strange decisions that seemed calculated to outrage the sensibilities of the American colonists. Ben, who loved to broker compromises, found that both sides were becoming increasingly stubborn. Parliament and Lord Townshend, the chancellor of the exchequer, or minister of finance, seemed determined to get money out of the colonists one way or another. And so they passed the Townshend Revenue Acts, which taxed glass, paper, paint, and tea. In response to the Townshend Acts, as the name was shortened to, American colonists once again refused to buy imported goods.

In the midst of all of this ongoing turmoil, Ben tried his best to get things done, but even he had to admit that he failed more times than he succeeded. He wrote to a friend about what he had observed in the British government. "The confusion among our Great Men still continues as great as ever. And a melancholy thing it is to consider, that instead of employing the present leisure of peace in such

measures as might extend our commerce, pay off
our debts, secure allies, and increase the strength
and ability of the nation to support a future war, the
whole time seems wasted in party contentions about
power and profit, in court intrigues and cabals, and
in abusing one another."

Not only did Ben bear the cares of the colonies
on his shoulders, but also he had personal worries.
Debby suffered a stroke and did not regain her
health, and then Sally wrote to say that she was
marrying a man named Richard Bache. Ben had
never met the man, who was a recent immigrant
from England, but he did not like the fact that
William had written to say that Richard had had
some money problems since arriving in Philadelphia.
Ben felt that Sally was taking a risk in marrying
Richard, and he refused to write a letter welcoming
Richard Bache into the family. But slowly Ben
adjusted to Sally's marriage to Richard, especially
when they produced a son, whom they named
Benjamin Franklin Bache, or Benny for short.

While he dealt with these family matters on the
other side of the Atlantic Ocean, he used the time
to get reacquainted with his grandson William
Temple, or just Temple, as everyone seemed to call
him, who had been living in England all this time.
Temple was now seven years old, and Ben had the
boy come and stay with him in London two or three
times a year. He thought that Temple was a polite
and intelligent boy with good potential to become a
prominent lawyer when he grew up.

Late in 1768 British troops had been sent to Boston, which seemed to the government in London to be the biggest trouble spot in the colonies, with orders to enforce the Townshend Acts and maintain order. At the time of the troops' departure, Ben had written to a friend, "The sending of soldiers to Boston always appeared to me a dangerous step; they could do no good, they might occasion mischief. I cannot but fear the consequences of bringing them together. It seems like setting up a smith's forge in a magazine of gunpowder."

Two of Ben's sister Jane's grandchildren had come from the colonies to stay with him, and Ben introduced them to London society. The children had brought with them newspapers from Boston that seemed to indicate that the gunpowder he spoke of was beginning to ignite. The newspapers carried reports of a melee between a number of residents of Boston and a group of British soldiers. The melee had turned deadly, with five Bostonians being shot and killed by bullets from the rifles of British soldiers. The whole deadly affair was now being referred to as the Boston Massacre.

Ben's heart sank as he read the accounts of the massacre. He hoped and prayed that this would be the only violent clash between the people of New England and the British soldiers. But given the stubbornness of both the colonists and members of the British parliament, Ben knew deep in his heart that the Boston Massacre was only the beginning.

Stepping Into the War

Over the next two years Ben did what he could to ease tensions between the various colonies and the British government, and he was able to help bring about some changes. In 1770 the Townshend Acts, which levied taxes on many items, had been repealed, but a tax on tea was left in place.

During this time someone handed Ben several letters from Thomas Hutchinson, the governor of Massachusetts. Although Ben did not ask where the letters had come from, he guessed that they had been stolen. In the letters Governor Hutchinson complained that the rebellious spirit in his colony was the work of a few men stirring things up. His remedy for this situation was for the British government to come down hard on the colonists so that they would remember their correct place.

Ben sent the letters off to representatives in Boston with explicit instructions that the letters were not to be published and should eventually be returned to him. Regrettably, his instructions were ignored, and the letters were published in Boston. Word of this got back to England, where many parliamentarians were furious. Several months later, when it was learned that Ben Franklin was the one who had sent the letters to Boston, they had a focus for their anger.

Sadly for Ben, the Hutchinson Letter Affair broke at the same time as a serious uprising in Boston. The event, which was soon being called the Boston Tea Party, came about as the result of the Tea Act, passed in 1773. While the American colonists had adjusted to the idea of paying taxes on tea, the British government went a step further and allowed the East India Company the exclusive right to ship and sell tea directly to the colonies. This meant that colonists could buy only East India Company tea and that merchants could no longer buy tea in England at the best price. Patriots, as those who supported the rights of the colonists over those of the crown were calling themselves, were furious. On the evening of December 16, 1773, fifty men disguised as Indians stormed the Boston dock and climbed aboard three East India Company ships carrying tea. They dragged chests of tea up from the holds of the ships and tipped them overboard. In all, 340 chests of tea worth nine thousand pounds were dumped into Boston Harbor.

Eight weeks later, when word of the Boston Tea Party reached England, there was an outcry against the colonists. Somehow the British had to get the message across that it was dangerous to challenge the mother country.

Right at that moment, Ben had to go before Parliament to answer charges related to the Hutchinson Letter Affair. As he took his place standing before the gathered members of Parliament, Ben felt the ugly mood in the building. His accusers stated that his purpose in leaking the letters was "to establish their [the colonists'] power, and make all future governors bow to their authority. They wish to erect themselves into a tyranny greater than the Roman; to be able, sitting in their own secret cabal, to dictate to the Assembly, and send away their...Governor...from his seat."

More accusations were made, including one that Ben had stirred up trouble because he wanted to be governor himself and that as a result *he* had organized the Boston Tea Party. Through it all, Ben stood silently, realizing that anything he said in response would only inflame the situation. Eight hours later, when the proceedings were over, Parliament took out their frustrations with the colonists on Ben, stripping him of his position as deputy postmaster general.

Ben was very angry at the outcome, both for himself and for the colonies. He was concerned that the British would never understand the colonists and would push them toward war. "Where complaining is a crime, hope becomes despair," he wrote, and he feared that the colonies were sinking into such despair.

Soon afterward, Parliament passed the Boston Port Act, which closed the Port of Boston to shipping until the residents of Boston repaid the East India Company for the tea that had been dumped into the harbor. Four other acts were also passed, all giving Great Britain more control over Massachusetts. These five acts became known as the Intolerable Acts. They were meant to punish Boston for the tea-tax protests, but what they actually did was incense many colonists up and down the eastern seaboard of North America.

In the weeks that followed the Boston Port Act, one colony after another agreed to send delegates to a special conference to be held in September in Philadelphia. The gathering was to be called the Continental Congress.

When Ben heard about the upcoming congress, he planned to be back in America in time to attend it himself. But the hope that he might have one last chance at bringing some reconciliation between the British and the American colonists kept him in England.

In January 1775 Ben received a letter that made him wish he had gone home earlier. The letter was from his son William, informing Ben of the bad news that Debby had suffered another stroke and died. Ben had not seen his wife for ten years, and now he would never see her again. It was a bitter moment for him and more so because he noticed in

William's letter hints that William had sided with the British and seemed ashamed of some of Ben's actions in London.

Three months later, when Ben could see no more chance of a compromise, he finally admitted defeat and booked a passage home for himself and his grandson Temple.

Temple was now fifteen years old, with a gift for languages and drawing. On the journey across the Atlantic, Ben engaged Temple's help in observing the ocean they were sailing across. Ben was still fascinated by why it took ships longer to sail from England to North America than it did going the other way. As they made their way across the Atlantic, he took careful measurements of the water. Part of this involved Temple's lowering a thermometer on a rope over the side of the ship at regular intervals and taking the temperature of the ocean water. What Ben learned from this was that at a certain point they sailed into a stretch of water that was nineteen degrees warmer than the water on either side of it. Ben noticed that this warmer water was a different color and did not sparkle at night the way the cooler water did. He also noticed that masses of seaweed, which the sailors referred to as gulfweed, floated in this warmer water.

As he talked more about the weed with the sailors, Ben learned that the weed seemed to float from the Caribbean Sea up the eastern coast of North America. As Ben thought about this and the observations and measurements he had made, he postulated that a large, warm ocean current flowed up the eastern seaboard of North America and then swung out into the Atlantic Ocean toward Great Britain. This would explain the phenomenon of ships going faster one way across the Atlantic Ocean than the other. On their way to England from the American colonies, the ships were sailing with the current. On the way back, they were sailing against the current, which slowed their progress.

In early May 1775 Ben arrived in New York, where he received a hero's welcome. He had been at sea for six weeks, and during this time when he was out of contact with the rest of the world, something huge had happened—the American Revolution had begun. Ben was stepping into the war he had for many years feared would eventually erupt.

Ben soon learned that on April 19 British soldiers had fought the patriots in the villages of Concord and Lexington, Massachusetts. The farmers and merchants in and around the villages had united into an army and repulsed the "redcoats," as the British soldiers were nicknamed.

Ben scarcely had time to introduce Temple to the family and get acquainted with Sally and Richard Bache's three children before he was elected as a delegate to the Second Continental Congress. At sixty-nine years of age, Ben was the oldest delegate present. The first congress had discussed plans to boycott products; this one discussed the preparations for war.

Ben was glad when the congress elected General George Washington as "Commander-in-Chief of the entire army of the United Colonies." He had first met George Washington twenty years before when he had helped supply General Braddock's army. Ben had been convinced then that George Washington had strong leadership skills, and he knew that he would need all of those skills and more in this present crisis. The odds against the colonists were great. The colonists had borders to defend with an army and a navy that had not yet been recruited. And once they did have a military, the new soldiers would need uniforms and weapons, food to eat, and horses and wagons to transport their supplies as they sought to overthrow the British and defend themselves against Indian attacks. And all of this would have to be achieved by thirteen separate colonies, each of which had different methods of government and, apart from uniting during the French and Indian War, had never before acted as a single unit.

Then there was the fact that many of the colonists were on the side of the British. They did not want a war. Ben was very aware of this circumstance because his own son William had declared himself to be a loyalist, siding with the British. The letter Ben wrote to William in response to his declaration that he was a loyalist was the most difficult letter he had ever written. Ben ended it by saying, "You will choose to remain loyal to your master, but I think independence more honorable than any service."

As he sent the letter to his son, Ben reflected on the terrible state of affairs in the colonies. Many other families besides his were divided, and now that an army and navy were being assembled, events had to end with a winner and a loser. If the patriots won, Ben would be part of a new country; if the British succeeded, he would lose everything he owned and very likely his head as well.

Although he was nearly seventy years old, Ben threw himself into the tasks that were given to him. He was once again elected to the Pennsylvania Assembly and put in charge of defending the colony. And as a member of the Continental Congress, he was asked to figure out where to get gunpowder for the army. Until now it had all been imported from England, but that was no longer possible.

In the meantime General George Washington had rushed to Boston, where patriot troops had surrounded the redcoats in the city. But before he got there, the British had captured Breed's Hill, in the process plundering and burning four hundred houses in Charlestown, across the Charles River from Boston, and killing many colonists.

As Ben followed the events, he felt sick to his stomach. Not only his son but also nearly every one of his English friends thought that the colonists were mad. In dismay and frustration, Ben wrote a letter to his old friend William Strahan, a member of Parliament in London. The letter, laced with bitterness, read:

Mr. Strahan:

You are a member of Parliament, and one of that majority which has doomed my country to destruction. You have begun to burn our towns and murder our people. Look upon your hands! They are stained with the blood of your relations! You and I were long friends. You are now my enemy, and I am

Yours,

B. Franklin

After penning the letter, Ben decided not to send it.

In October 1775 Ben and two other delegates were sent to Cambridge, Massachusetts, to meet with General Washington. Their task was to help Washington come up with ways to supply the new Continental Army. It was a huge task, since Washington wanted his army to consist of twenty thousand volunteers who would each enlist for one year. Ben set to work finding food, blankets, and tents for these new soldiers.

It soon became clear that the British planned to use Canada, their newest colony in North America, as a staging ground for their attacks on the rebellious colonies to the south. A patriot force under the command of Colonel Benedict Arnold was sent north to try to capture Canada and deny the British their staging ground. The force managed to capture Montreal but failed miserably when it tried to capture the city of Quebec. The Continental Congress decided to try a different approach. In March 1776 a commission was appointed to travel north to Canada to try to convince the former residents of New France to side with the other colonies and oust their new overlords from North America. The commission comprised Samuel Chase and Charles Carroll of Maryland, and Ben Franklin.

Seventy-year-old Ben now suffered from gout, and the journey north to Canada was difficult. For twenty-seven days the men traveled on horseback north along the Hudson River and then along the edge of Lake Champlain, before making it into Canada. It was March, and the conditions were frigid. Snow blanketed the ground, and ice made the trail dangerous to travel along. Ben's body ached, and at times he wondered whether he was going to make it alive to Canada.

All the members of the commission did make it to Canada alive, but once they got there, they wondered why they had bothered to make such a treacherous journey. Nearly all of the eighty thousand French residents of Canada were Catholic, and they were well aware of the prejudice against Catholics in the other American colonies. As a result, they were not willing to give up the religious freedom they enjoyed to join with the other colonies to fight the British.

Ben was relieved that the traveling was over when he finally arrived back in Philadelphia after the arduous journey to Canada. A new appointment also awaited him. The leaders of the Continental Congress realized that their success in defeating the British would depend on the support of other European countries, especially England's archenemy, France. As a result, Ben was appointed to a secret committee whose job it was to write to their various contacts in Europe and sound them out regarding their countries' attitudes toward what was happening in America and whether their governments might in some way be willing to help the patriots in the war effort.

When Ben had been in London several years before, he had met Thomas Paine. Thomas had an inquiring mind, and the two men had struck up an acquaintance. In 1774, when Thomas told Ben that he had decided to emigrate to the colonies, Ben wrote a letter of introduction for him. He addressed the letter to his son-in-law, Richard Bache, and asked him to help find Thomas a job and get him established in Philadelphia. Ben was delighted that once he arrived in the colonies, Thomas had found his calling in life as a writer. Ben was even more delighted now. In January 1776 Thomas Paine had published a book titled *Common Sense.* The book attacked England, pointing out that it made no sense for the colonies to stay connected to Great Britain. Like a child who grows and leaves home, it was time for the American colonies to have a government of their own. And that government should not only be independent of Great Britain but be a representative form of democracy. "A government of our own is our natural right," Thomas boldly declared. The book struck a chord with people, so much so that 150,000 copies of it had soon been sold. Ben was amazed. As a former printer, he knew that this was a staggering number of books to sell.

As they read *Common Sense,* people in the colonies began to take up the cry for independence. Even people who had been on the fence regarding the issue were now siding with the patriots. In response to the public clamor for independence, on June 7, 1776, Richard Henry Lee, a delegate from Virginia, introduced a resolution to the Continental Congress. The resolution declared that "these united colonies are, and of right ought to be, free and independent states, that they are absolved from all allegiance to the British Crown, and that all political connection between them and the State of Great Britain is, and ought to be, totally dissolved."

Some of the delegates to the congress, especially those from New York, New Jersey, and Delaware, showed some reluctance regarding the bold declaration. They wanted more time to think about it, and so a final vote on the matter was put off until July 1. But the congress did establish a committee to draft a Declaration of Independence, which would lay out in careful detail why the colonies had decided to declare their independence from Great Britain. Appointed to the committee to draft the Declaration of Independence were John Adams of Massachusetts, Thomas Jefferson of Virginia, Roger Sherman of Connecticut, Robert Livingston of New York, and Ben Franklin.

The committee quickly got to work, though in truth Ben had little to do with producing the first draft of the document. He left that task to Thomas Jefferson. "You can write ten times better than I," he told Jefferson.

When Jefferson had finished writing the first draft of the document, he sent it to Ben with a cover note that read, "Will Doctor Franklin be so good as to peruse it and suggest such alterations as his more enlarged view of the subject will dictate?"

Ben read the draft of the Declaration of Independence. He was impressed at the job Jefferson had done, and most of the changes he suggested revolved around more specific wording.

When the Declaration of Independence was laid before the Continental Congress, the members of the congress were much harsher with the document than Ben had been. Clauses and whole sentences were edited from the declaration as Jefferson looked on ashen-faced.

Ben could clearly see the shock Jefferson was in as his prized document was changed and edited before his very eyes. He reached over and tried to cheer Jefferson up by telling him one of his anecdotes. He told him about a certain hatter named John Thompson, who had gone into business and put a new sign over his door. The sign included a picture of a hat and, underneath, the words "John Thompson, Hatter, makes and sells hats for ready money." By the time his friends had edited his words, the sign had been reduced to nothing but the picture of the hat with "John Thompson" below it. "As a result," Ben said, "whenever in my power, I try to avoid becoming the draughtsman of papers to be reviewed by a public body."

Finally a smile spread across Jefferson's pale face.

On July 4, 1776, after three days of debating and editing the Declaration of Independence, the Continental Congress voted to adopt the document.

On August 2 the delegates to the congress gathered to affix their signatures to a parchment copy of the Declaration of Independence. When they were done, John Hancock, the president of the congress, declared to the delegates, "There must be no pulling different ways. We must all hang together."

"Yes, we must indeed all hang together, or most assuredly we shall all hang separately," Ben quipped in response.

With independence declared, Pennsylvania felt that it was no longer a proprietorship. The Penn family's hold over the colony had been broken, and it was now time to draft a new constitution for the colony. Ben was soon put to work helping out with this process.

Soon after the Declaration of Independence had been signed, two hundred British warships landed thirty thousand soldiers on the western end of Long Island to engage George Washington's Continental Army. The superior British force soon overwhelmed Washington's men, and it was only a daring retreat across the East River to Manhattan Island in the dead of night that saved the patriots from total annihilation. From Manhattan, Washington's army had retreated into New Jersey, and the British had set up their military headquarters on Staten Island. From there Admiral Lord Howe, the British military commander and old friend of Ben's, proposed a peace conference. Ben, along with John Adams and Edmund Rutledge, was sent by the Continental Congress to meet with Lord Howe.

The three men arrived at the stately Billopp House in Tottenville, on Staten Island, on September 11, 1776. Admiral Lord Howe and his brother, General Richard Howe, warmly greeted Ben and his two companions and showed them the utmost respect and hospitality. However, it soon became obvious to Ben and the others that no progress toward peace could be made. All Lord Howe had to offer was a promise from King George III of pardon for any rebel who said he was sorry, and before any further peace negotiations could be entered into, the Declaration of Independence would have to be revoked. Such conditions were completely unacceptable to Ben and the other representatives of the Continental Congress, and the meeting soon broke up.

When Ben arrived back in Philadelphia, he learned that the congress had appointed a commission to negotiate a treaty of alliance with the French. Ben was surprised to learn that along with Silas Deane and Arthur Lee, he had been appointed to the commission. The other two men were already abroad, and Ben would meet them in Paris. Seventy-year-old Ben Franklin was once again on his way across the Atlantic Ocean.

Chapter 16

Minister to France

Since he was an old man now, Ben Franklin decided that he should set his affairs in order before he left for France. He wrote a will and left his personal papers with a friend for safekeeping. Then he loaned the Continental Congress several thousand pounds before climbing aboard the *Reprisal*, a fast but cramped sloop, for the trip across the Atlantic Ocean to France. Traveling with Ben were two of his grandsons, Temple and seven-year-old Benny Bache. Benny was to start school in Europe, while Temple would serve as Ben's secretary. Ben had another reason for taking Temple with him; he wanted to keep the boy away from the influence of his father, who, much to Ben's chagrin, was a diehard loyalist—so much so that William Franklin was now under house arrest as a spy in Connecticut after it was discovered that he had been supplying the British with secret information.

On October 26, 1776, as the *Reprisal* left the Delaware River behind and sailed out into the Atlantic Ocean, Ben stood on deck and watched as the sun set over the American continent. Many of his friends were now dead, and he wondered whether he would ever see the sun setting over North America again. And if he did return from France, would it be a free nation he returned to, or would it be back under the thumb of the British? The answer to the question he supposed depended on the success of his mission to France. Would he be able to convince the French to side with the Americans and supply them with badly needed weapons?

As they headed across the Atlantic, Ben and Temple once again busied themselves observing the ocean and taking the temperature of the seawater at regular intervals. Ben was eager to find the extent of the current that appeared to flow all the way up from the Caribbean Sea and out across the North Atlantic.

The *Reprisal* was a swift ship, and much to Ben's surprise and delight, four weeks later the coast of France came into view. While the voyage had been eventful, Ben was glad to see land. For some reason, on this voyage he had become seasick, causing him to have to spend whole days on his bunk below deck. He was looking forward to getting his feet back on dry land. However, before the ship docked, an adventure awaited. Near the French coast, the captain of the *Reprisal* spotted two small British merchant ships. He gave chase, capturing both of the British vessels in the name of the Continental Congress.

Finally, on December 3, 1776, Ben Franklin and his two grandsons docked in France. After disembarking, they boarded a coach for the 320-mile journey to Paris. Ben felt terrible as he bumped along in the coach while his two grandsons peered out the window at the passing countryside.

By the time he got to Paris, Ben felt too ill to dress up, so he wore his simplest clothes, including a fur cap and a plain, brown coat. He was also too old to care about vanity, so he wore his glasses in public, something no one else ever did, and he did not wear his wig, because it irritated his head. And when he went out, he leaned on a length of crabtree that had been whittled into a walking stick for him in Philadelphia. This was a complete contrast to the French fashion of lace, ruffles, and elaborate wigs, even for men.

Much to his astonishment, the French loved Ben and his plain ways. They called him a true American, plain dressed and plain speaking. Instantly Ben found himself the toast of Paris. Everyone, it seemed, wanted an engraving of him either on their mantelpiece or in a locket around their necks. Ben wrote home to his sister that his image was just as recognizable in Paris as that of the moon. Ben decided to use whatever fame his simple garb brought him to advance the American cause.

When Ben finally arrived at the royal palace at Versailles, on the outskirts of Paris, he was greeted by Silas Deane, who had mixed news to tell him. The good news was that Silas had persuaded the French government to secretly sell the Americans hundreds of thousands of pounds of gunpowder. In addition, King Louis XVI of France had set up a secret dummy company in conjunction with his uncle, King Charles III of Spain. This company would send arms to a Dutch port in the Caribbean, where American ships would pick them up in exchange for rice, indigo, and tobacco. The bad news was that Silas had made little headway with the king of France or his court. Ben was not surprised. Back in Connecticut, Silas had been a schoolmaster. He was not used to dealing with the royal courts of Europe, which were complex and filled with intrigue.

Silas reported that while the king of France was willing to secretly help the patriot cause, he was not yet ready to openly support the American colonists and declare war on Britain, at least not until he was convinced that the Americans would win the war. He did not want to be seen openly backing the losing side, so until he was so convinced, everything would have to be done in secret.

This put Ben and Silas in a predicament. They knew that they needed French support to win the war, but the French were unwilling to offer that support until victory was assured.

Arthur Lee joined the other two commissioners in Paris just before Christmas, and all three men agreed that the situation was dismal. Every piece of news that arrived from America seemed more depressing than the previous piece, especially news about the fighting. Things did not appear to be going well for George Washington.

Ben walked a narrow line in his dealings with the royal court. He hinted to the French that the colonists might have to make peace with Great Britain, thus strengthening the British Empire once again, while making it also seem that the patriots had what it took to continue the fight.

Then, in early February 1777, better news arrived. On Christmas Day, Washington had led his Continental Army across the Delaware River and mounted a daring surprise attack on the British wintering over in Trenton, New Jersey. The patriots had won the fight and captured nearly one thousand prisoners of war. The news cheered Ben a great deal, and he went straightaway to share it with the Comte de Vergennes, the French foreign minister, with whom he had struck up a warm friendship. He hoped that the information would inch the French government closer to open support of the Americans.

Meanwhile Ben moved from the hotel where he had been staying into a suite of rooms at Passy, a small village two miles outside of Paris. At the same time, he sent Benny off to Switzerland to attend school.

With each passing day in Ben's new accommodations at Passy, strangers would show up at the door imploring Ben to set things up so that they

could join in the Revolutionary War against Britain.
The Marquis de Lafayette wanted to avenge the
death of his father at the hands of the British in the
French and Indian Wars. Others, like Baron von
Steuben, were professional soldiers looking for a
theater of operations within which to practice their
military skills.

At first Ben welcomed these men, because one
thing the Americans lacked was capable military
leaders. When the colonies had been under British
rule, the English had supplied nearly all of the military officers, with the American colonists serving as
the foot soldiers in makeshift armies. However, the
flood of hopeful soldiers, all of whom wanted to be
guaranteed some high rank in the Continental
Army, soon grew to be a problem. George Washington finally wrote to Ben, urging him not to send
over any more Europeans.

While Ben knew he could not stop adventurous
Europeans from traveling to America to join in the
war, he devised a diplomatic way not to recommend
them for service of high rank. He composed a
generic letter of reference that he gave to anyone
who asked him for a letter of introduction across
the Atlantic Ocean. The letter read:

Sir:
The bearer of this who is going to America
presses me to give him a letter of recommen-
dation, though I know nothing of him, not
even his name. This may seem extraordinary, but I assure you it is not uncommon

here. Sometimes indeed one unknown person brings me another equally unknown, to recommend him; and sometimes they recommend one another! As to this gentlemen, I must refer you to himself for his character and merits, with which he is certainly better acquainted than I can possibly be.

All the while, Ben kept busy trying to convince the French king and his lords that George Washington and his troops could win the war. Then finally, in October 1777, Ben received the news he needed. The patriots had fought and won the Battle of Saratoga, and 5,800 British soldiers had been taken captive, along with huge quantities of guns and ammunition. Now the French believed that the colonists could really win the war, and in February 1778 Ben signed the Treaty of Alliance on behalf of the American people. The treaty guaranteed that France would fight for the "liberty, sovereignty, and independence, absolute and unlimited, of the United States."

A month later Ben and his fellow American commissioners were officially presented to King Louis XVI at the royal palace in Versailles.

The Congress in Philadelphia ratified the treaty with France in May, and in September 1778 Ben was appointed to the position of minister to France.

Now that he was the officially recognized minister to France, Ben began moving more freely in French society. He started attending the opera and the theater, where he was often openly applauded. He also attended the salons that various well-connected and well-to-do women held in their homes. On one occasion Ben attended a meeting of the Royal Society of Science at which the French author and philosopher Voltaire was in attendance. When the audience learned that the two men had never met, they insisted that the two of them publicly greet each other. Ben and Voltaire embraced and kissed each other on the cheeks in French style, and the audience went wild with applause.

Ben's role as minister to France kept him busy negotiating loans with France and other European countries to finance George Washington and his Continental Army, who were still locked in mortal combat with the British. These negotiations were not always easy, since the United States was a country in name only. It had no firm central government but was just a group of separate colonies trying to act together as best they could. However, Ben, in his understated manner, was very persuasive, and soon money for arms and other supplies began to flow across the Atlantic from Europe.

Finally, in July 1780 the French sent General Rochambeau and five thousand troops to America to assist George Washington. And the next year a powerful naval force under the command of Admiral de Grasse was dispatched across the Atlantic to help with the fighting.

Ben hoped and prayed that these French forces would help turn the tide in the war. He was overjoyed when he learned in November 1781 that they had. British General Charles Cornwallis had surrendered his army to George Washington and his combined French and American army at Yorktown, Virginia. Ben was even more delighted when he learned the important role the French had played in the battle. The French naval force had blockaded Chesapeake Bay so that Cornwallis's army could not be reinforced; and General Rochambeau, a master at the art of siege, had coordinated the eight-day siege of the British army at Yorktown. Trapped at the end of the York peninsula with no way of escape, General Cornwallis had had no other option but to surrender his army to George Washington. On October 19, 1781, 7,250 British soldiers and 850 sailors formally surrendered themselves and their 244 cannons to Washington. Ben hoped that this stunning defeat would bring the British to their senses and that the war would soon be over.

Sure enough, early in 1782 Ben learned that the British had had enough. Deeply in debt because of the war effort and unable to raise more volunteers to fight, British Prime Minister Lord North had sent word to Philadelphia that England was ready to make peace with her former colonies. John Jay and John Adams were dispatched to France by the Continental Congress to help Ben negotiate a peace treaty with the British.

The men who made up the American delegation all had strong personalities and firm but differing ideas of what a peace treaty should contain. As a result, tensions often ran high among them, and especially between Ben and John Adams. Ben thought that Adams was too high-strung. Adams was all business and seemed to find it hard to relax and enjoy himself once in a while. Ben even commented in a letter home that John Adams "means well for his country, is always an honest man, often a wise one, but sometimes, and in some things, absolutely out of his senses." Despite these interpersonal conflicts and ambitions, Ben did not lose sight of the greater goal of seeing the fledgling United States firmly established and recognized as a legitimate nation. And whether the other men chose to acknowledge it or not, he was the member of the delegation with the most diplomatic experience. Ben used his knowledge and experience to the delegation's benefit, negotiating a treaty to the full benefit of the United States.

September 3, 1783, was a proud day for Ben as he gathered at Versailles with John Jay and John Adams, along with David Hartley, King George III's official representative, to formally affix their signatures to the Treaty of Paris, which officially ended the war with Great Britain. The first sentence of the treaty declared, "His Britannic Majesty acknowledges the said United States...to be free, sovereign and independent states."

After the treaty had been negotiated and signed, Ben asked Congress to recall him back to the United States. But Ben was an able negotiator, and the congress was in no hurry to release him. Now that the United States was truly a free and independent country, new commercial treaties needed to be negotiated with other European countries, and Ben was the perfect man for the job.

Ben threw himself into this new task. It was while he was negotiating and writing these new treaties that he grew weary of having to change glasses. For some time now he had carried two pairs of glasses with him, one pair to help him see distances and the other pair to help him read and see things close up. But constantly having to change glasses was a frustration, so Ben took both pairs to a glasscutter and asked him to cut the lenses in half horizontally. Ben then glued the bottom of the distance lenses to the top of the close-up lenses and reinserted them into the frame. Now when he looked up, he could see distances, and when he looked down, he could see close up. Much to his delight, he no longer had to switch between two pairs of glasses.

Finally, in May 1785 Congress allowed Ben to return to Philadelphia and sent Thomas Jefferson to replace him in France. Ben was touched by the great compliment Jefferson paid him. Jefferson made it clear to everyone that he was Ben's successor, not his replacement, for, he said, "no one could replace Benjamin Franklin."

By now Ben was seventy-nine years old, his health was frail, and he had difficulty walking. He took to being carried around in a sedan chair. Despite his age and infirmity, Ben had made an impact on the French, who did not want him to leave their country. And after nine years in their country, Ben had grown to love and respect the French. But at heart he was an American, and despite the French warmth and hospitality toward him, he looked forward to getting back to his beloved Philadelphia. The king provided transportation to take Ben to the port of Le Havre. Traveling with Ben were his two grandsons, Temple and Benny. As the procession wound its way toward Le Havre in July 1785, people lined the roadside to honor and bid farewell to Ben Franklin and throw flowers in his path. Ben was deeply touched by their sentiment.

From France Ben sailed across the English Channel to Southampton, England, for a reunion with his son William. After being released from house arrest in Connecticut in a prisoner exchange, William had eventually made his way to England to live. Although Ben had no problem forgiving and forgetting the fact that most of his English friends had sided with the British Crown during the Revolutionary War, he found it impossible to forget what his son had done. He felt deeply hurt by what he saw as William's treasonous actions during the war, and their meeting together in Southampton was tense. Ben knew that his son wanted to be reconciled to him; William had written to him in France expressing that desire. But somehow Ben could not do it. In his eyes the fault lay with William, and their relationship could never again be as it had been.

After several days in England, Temple and Benny helped their grandfather aboard ship. From the deck of the vessel, Ben watched the sun set. His thoughts turned to the future. He had left Philadelphia nine years before, when the outcome of the

war was uncertain. Now as he returned to his home-
land, he was returning to a new country—the
United States—which finally had a certain future,
or so he thought.

Chapter 17

A Useful Life

A cheering throng of citizens greeted Ben as he was helped off the ship onto the Market Street wharf. After being officially welcomed home, he made his way to his house, where Sally and Richard and his grandchildren now lived. With great satisfaction Ben wrote in his journal that evening, "We landed at Market Street wharf, where we were received by a crowd of people with huzzas, and accompanied with acclamations quite to my door. Found my family well. God be praised and thanked for all His mercies!"

Over the next few weeks Ben got reacquainted with his six other grandchildren and renewed some of his old friendships. Since many of his friends had died in the nine years he had been away, he contented himself visiting the children and grandchildren of many of his old friends.

Ben's mind was as active as ever, and he busied himself landscaping his yard and writing letters to his friends around the world. He also built a new wing onto the family home and drew up plans for a rental house next door. He tried to make this second house as fireproof as possible. He designed the house so that the wooden frame of each room did not touch the frame of the next room, and the floors and stairs were all plastered over. Trapdoors allowed easy access to the roof in case of fire. Ben envisaged firemen being able to climb through the trapdoors to douse the fire from above.

Now in his old age, the Revolutionary War was well behind Ben. He had returned home hoping that he would be able to spend his last days writing, reading, and visiting, but duty called him yet again. No sooner had Ben settled into his house than he was made president of Pennsylvania's Supreme Council, the equivalent of the prewar assembly. Ben did not have the heart to refuse the post, especially when he realized just how much delegates with common sense were needed. During the war many patriot leaders had given a great deal of thought to how to win the war, but now that there was peace, no one seemed quite sure what to do next. Each of the thirteen colonies was acting as a sovereign, independent unit, with little commitment to becoming a union. As time went on, it became obvious that some kind of union was necessary. A central government was needed for defense and to make trade agreements.

By May 1787 things had become so bad that each colony, except for Rhode Island, agreed to send delegates to a special convention at the Pennsylvania State House. Fifty-five men showed up, most of them were half Ben's age or younger. Ben had to be carried to the State House in the sedan chair he had brought back from France. Convicts from a nearby prison were enlisted to carry it. Once he had been delivered to the State House, Ben could walk only a few steps or stand for a minute or so. Even with these physical handicaps, Ben worked untiringly to see that George Washington was elected president of the convention. The other delegates at the convention were in awe of Ben at times, but when the debates got heated, they attacked him just as vehemently as they did the other delegates. At times, when the doors were closed, the convention became very ugly.

Two issues were particularly contentious. The first had to do with slavery. Ben had changed his view on slavery over the years, and in his old age he had come to believe that the practice was out of step with the spirit of liberty sweeping the country. He wondered how citizens could embrace the wording of a constitution that declared that all men were created equal without acknowledging that black slaves deserved the same rights as everyone else.

After arriving back from Paris, Ben had become president of the Pennsylvania Society for Promoting the Abolition of Slavery. In June 1787 the society adopted a petition that urged the Constitutional Convention to "make the suppression of the African slave trade in the United States a part of their important deliberations." However, the southern states were heavily involved in agriculture and insisted that they needed slaves to work in the fields. These states said that they would form their own country before they would submit to freeing slaves.

It became clear to Ben and to the others who wanted to have slavery abolished in the United States that there would be no union unless the plan to ban slavery was dropped for the present. Ben was bitterly disappointed, but he did push for some changes in the laws. Eventually it was agreed that slavery would continue to be legal in the southern states, but in twenty years' time, the importing of slaves from Africa would be banned. After that time, new slaves would have to be born in the United States. Ben predicted that the issue of slavery would one day come back to haunt the United States.

The second issue had to do with who should make up the representative arm of the new government. Should the states with the largest populations have more say, or the ones with the largest land area?

After listening to four months of heated arguments on the matter, Ben used a simple example to encourage the delegates to compromise:

> When a broad table is to be made, and the edges of the planks do not fit, the artist takes a little from both, and makes a good joint. In like manner here both sides must part with some of their demands, in order that they may join in some accommodating proposition.

Eventually the convention delegates followed Ben's urging and compromised. On the issue of state representation, Congress, the new representative arm of government, was divided into two separate houses, the Senate and the House of Representatives. Each state would have the same number of delegates in the Senate, but the number of delegates each state had in the House of Representatives would differ, depending upon the population of each particular state.

When everything was decided, Ben concluded with a speech that he wrote, which was read for him by James Wilson:

> I agree to this Constitution, with all its faults, if they are such; because I think a general government necessary for us, and there is no form of government but what may be a blessing to the people if well administered; and I believe further that this is likely to be well administered for a course of years, and can only end in despotism, as other forms have done before it, when the people shall become so corrupted as to need despotic government, being incapable of any other.
>
> I doubt, too, whether any other convention we can obtain may be able to make a better Constitution; for when you assemble a number of men to have the advantage of their joint wisdom, you inevitably assemble with those men all their prejudices, their passions, their errors of opinion, their local

interests, and their selfish views. From such an assembly can a perfect production be expected? It therefore astonishes me, Sir, to find this system approaching so near to perfection as it does; and I think it will astonish our enemies, who are waiting with confidence to hear that our councils are confounded, like those of the builders of Babel, and that our states are on the point of separation, only to meet hereafter for the purpose of cutting one another's throats....

On the whole, Sir, I cannot help expressing a wish that every member of the convention, who may still have objections to it, would with me on this occasion doubt a little of his own infallibility, and to make *manifest* our *unanimity*, put his name to this Instrument.

Forty of the forty-two delegates present at the signing of the Constitution of the United States of America affixed their signatures to the document, including, of course, Ben Franklin. In signing it, Ben became the only man to sign all five of the most important documents upon which the United States was built: the Declaration of Independence, the Treaty of Amity and Commerce with France, the Treaty of Alliance with France, the Treaty of Peace with England (Treaty of Paris), and the Constitution of the United States.

On April 14, 1789, the new Congress unanimously chose George Washington to be the first president of the United States, and on April 30,

Washington took the oath of office on the balcony of
the Federal Hall in New York City. Of the occasion
Ben wrote, "Our grand machine has at length
begun to work. I pray God to bless and guide its
operations. If any form of government is capable of
making a nation happy, ours I think bids fair now
for producing that effect. But after all, much
depends upon the people who are to be governed."

· Not long after the signing of the constitution,
Ben slipped on a stone step outside his house,
falling and badly bruising himself. He never fully
recovered from the accident and afterward was
forced to spend a good deal of his time in bed.

Despite his frail health, three things kept Ben's
spirits up: visitors from around the world, his huge
library, and his eight grandchildren. By now Benny
Bache was a young printer, and Ben was proud to
think that Benny was following in the footsteps of
his grandfather.

As the new decade of the 1790s dawned, Ben
knew he could not live much longer, and so he
revised his will. He left much of his wealth to the
Pennsylvania Hospital and a thousand pounds
each to Boston and Philadelphia to fund young
tradesmen setting out in business. He also had
plenty of money left over for his daughter, Sally,
and her husband, Richard, and for his grandchildren. To his son William, Ben left his books and
papers and some lands in Canada, but no money,
feeling that if his loyalist son had had his way and
England had won the war, Ben would have had no
inheritance to leave at all. Ben decided to leave his

crabtree walking stick to his good friend George Washington. It seemed hard to believe that he had first met Washington thirty-five years before when they were both loyal citizens of Great Britain.

Finally, on the night of April 17, 1790, eighty-four-year-old Benjamin Franklin knew that he was close to death. He rallied enough strength to climb out of bed and asked Sally to change his sheets so that he could die "in a decent manner." As Ben climbed back into bed, pain overcame him. He winced, and Sally said, "Papa, I hope you will be better soon and live for many more years."

"I hope not," Ben replied.

Then Temple suggested that he roll over a little to make breathing easier for him.

"A dying man can do nothing easily," Ben observed.

These were the last words that Ben Franklin spoke. Ben drifted into a coma soon afterward and died at eleven o'clock that evening with his grandsons Temple and Benny standing at his bedside. On news of his death, bells all over Philadelphia tolled, and flags were lowered to half-staff.

Four days later Philadelphia hosted the biggest funeral ever held up to that time in the colonies or in the United States. Twenty thousand people watched respectfully as Ben Franklin was laid to rest at Christ Church between his wife, Debby, and their son Francis.

As news of Ben's death spread around the world, so did the mourning. Ben was lauded by Congress as "a citizen whose native genius was not more an ornament to human nature than his various exertions of it have been precious to science, to freedom and to his country." The French government declared, "Franklin is dead! The genius, that freed America and poured a flood of light over Europe, has returned to the bosom of the Divinity.... A man is dead and two worlds mourn."

It was a good thing that Ben was not around to hear the praise; he would have been embarrassed by such acclaim. He really wanted to be remembered for only one thing, and he had stated that in a letter home to his mother years before: "I would rather have it said, 'He lived usefully' than 'He died rich.'"

Ben's amazingly rich legacy can leave no doubt that Ben Franklin accomplished his goal: he lived *a useful life.*

Aldridge, Alfred Owen. *Benjamin Franklin: Philosopher and Man*. Philadelphia: J. B. Lippincott, 1965.

Brands, H. W. *The First American: The Life and Times of Benjamin Franklin*. New York: Doubleday, 2000.

Fleming, Candace. *Ben Franklin's Almanac: Being a True Account of the Good Gentleman's Life*. New York: Atheneum Books for Young Readers, 2003.

Lopez, Claude-Anne, and Eugenia W. Herbert. *The Private Franklin: The Man and His Family*. New York: W. W. Norton, 1975.

Meltzer, Milton. *Benjamin Franklin: The New American*. New York: Franklin Watts, 1988.

Srodes, James. *Franklin: The Essential Founding Father*. Washington, D.C.: Regnery Publishing, 2002.

Wright, Esmond. *Franklin of Philadelphia*. Cambridge: The Belknap Press of Harvard University Press, 1986.

Janet and Geoff Benge are a husband and wife writing team with twenty years of writing experience. Janet is a former elementary school teacher. Geoff holds a degree in history. Together they have a passion to make history come alive for a new generation of readers.

Originally from New Zealand, the Benges make their home in the Orlando, Florida, area.

Also from Janet and Geoff Benge...

More adventure-filled biographies for ages 10 to 100!

Elisabeth Elliot: Joyful Surrender • 978-1-57658-513-9
Paul Brand: Helping Hands • 978-1-57658-536-8
D. L. Moody: Bringing Souls to Christ • 978-1-57658-552-8
Dietrich Bonhoeffer: In the Midst of Wickedness • 978-1-57658-713-3
Francis Asbury: Circuit Rider • 978-1-57658-737-9
Samuel Zwemer: The Burden of Arabia • 978-1-57658-738-6

All titles are available as e-books. Audiobooks and Unit Study
Curriculum Guides are available for select biographies.

Visit www.ywampublishing.com or call 1-800-922-2143.